MW00440501

An Evil Day

Forgiving, Forgetting, and Moving on
When Life's Darkest Moments
Leave You with Nothing

GEORGE PANTAGES

George Pantages Ministries

Copyright © 2007 by George Pantages

An Evil Day
by George Pantages

Printed in the United States of America

ISBN 978-1-60266-342-8

All rights reserved solely by the author.

The author guarantees all contents are original and do not infringe upon the legal rights of any other person or work.

No part of this book may be reproduced in any form without the permission of the author.

Unless otherwise indicated, Bible quotations are taken from NKJV. Copyright © 2006 by Thomas Nelson.

KJV. Copyright © 2006 by Thomas Nelson.

Dedication

This book is dedicated to two special people that helped me through my evil day. First of all, my mom, Amelia Gomez, who passed away last year (2006) in March. Little did she know that all the turmoil that she endured in her own marriage was only to prepare her to counsel her number one son when he needed it most.

With a literal shoulder to cry on, she walked me through the most heart-wrenching experiences that anyone could ever imagine. I'm sorry that you weren't around to see the finished product, but just to let you know, you were my inspiration. Thanks, Mom, for all your help and encouragement. I could not have done it without you. See you in heaven!

The second person that I would like to acknowledge is my son Timothy (Buster). During the break-up with his mom, he was always at my side, even though he was hurting just as much if not more so than me. He was the only one to see me at my worst, and, like the Lord, still loves me. Thanks, Buster, for never quitting on your dad.

My Deepest Appreciation to...

My three children Timothy, Stephanie, and Christi. You are the greatest treasure a father could ever have. All of you touch me so differently and so profoundly that living without you would be unthinkable.

The men of God that helped me through the "evil day":

Pastor Joe Aguilar, Pastor Obed Aguilar, Bishop Julian Aguirre, Pastor Lupito Arroyo, Pastor Richard Galaviz, Pastor Benjamín Guerra, Bishop Daniel Jauhall, Pastor Ignacio Leon, Pastor Richard Meza, Bishop Samuel Valverde

The precious women that helped edit and translate this book, Diana Alvarez, Kim Smith and Dannia Yepiz.
Your help was truly invaluable.

CONTACT INFORMATION

George Pantages Ministries

George Pantages
Cell 512 785-6324
geopanjr@yahoo.com
Georgepantages.com

Table of Contents

Introduction

It is amazing how we can read, hear, or even study scripture over and over again and yet never truly understand its correct meaning. Why is it when our world has been turned upside down that the precious nuggets that have been hidden for years suddenly come to light? Is it just human nature that restricts our search for the deeper things in God, as we casually study the Scriptures? Are God's abundant blessings the cause for our stunted growth in Him?

For all that that Job appeared to be before all was taken away, his relationship with God was not complete. He only knew a God of prosperity. One that caused him to see others not as blessed to be somewhat lacking in their relationship with God. His pride blinded him to the other wonderful attributes that God had to offer. It was only after the dust had settled, having all his earthly possessions restored again, that he makes a startling statement. Job 42:5: *"I have heard of You by the hearing of the ear, but now my eye sees You."*

Far too long we have been hearing about a God that continues to create and recreate. The stories seem so incredible and so way out there because they appear to happen only to those who have suffered great, great losses. What makes it even more mind-boggling is that God would do such a thing for a person who, in our minds, has brought it upon themselves. The Lord is not concerned about how we arrive at our losses, neither should we be. The most important thing about surviving an evil day is that the Lord has the solution, and if we can step out by faith, He is there to give us what we need.

Chapter 1
I Just Don't Understand

And the peace of God, which passeth all understanding,
shall keep your hearts and minds through Christ Jesus.
                                                    Philippians 4:7 KJV

On Halloween day, at the age of five, I came home from school sick very sick. Within a week's time, I was completely paralyzed and was rushed to General Hospital in Los Angeles, California. My family's life changed forever. Many years have since passed, but the need to know what really took place during my adolescent years prompted me to pursue the truth about what my parents went through and how their decisions affected my life as an adult. There was much I just didn't understand. I had many questions throughout my life that had gone unanswered. With a sense of urgency, I needed to find answers. My mom shared her perspective with me when I was old enough to insist. This is what she told me one Sunday evening after coming home from church. I remember the day as if it were yesterday. "You may have been too young to remember, Junior, but when you were just a boy, too young to be in school, your father had received the calling to the serve in the ministry. We thought he would accept, but instead he decided to pursue his career. We became "Domingueros," you know, going to church only on Sundays. His career became first, and money became his god. It was easy to get sucked into the pleasures of materialistic niceties. We lived in a new home furnished with the best furniture. We had a new car, and you kids were the best dressed children on the block.

"I was soon to find out that money didn't buy happiness. We had everything one could possibly want success, money, a call to the ministry, and a wonderful family; yet it didn't stop your father from finding someone else to love. His infidelity started a barrage of attacks from hell's gate from which, even to this day, we all are still trying to recover. After he left the family and moved out, I discovered that many of the bills had not been paid, and that there would be a great possibility I'd lose the house. To make matters worse, I had not worked one day in the eight years of our marriage so that I could stay home and raise our children. Never in my wildest dreams did I believe your father would want another life.

"To make matters worse, I had no skills, and finding a job at the time was a challenge and almost unbearable. There was little to no time to go to church, and I knew it was wrong. I wanted to die, but it was my children who sustained my will to live. All this was going on when you came home from school sick that Halloween day. With each day that passed, you became sicker and sicker. I tried every home remedy I could think of, and nothing helped. After one week, I took you to the hospital. Your Grandpa Frank came to pray for you. He prophesied and admonished me to trust in God and not to worry that you were going to be coming out of the hospital alive, and the confirmation would be that physically everything was going to be normal except for a withered right arm. Even though I knew God was able to heal you and keep you from death, to trust in Him and believe what I was told was probably the hardest thing I had ever had to do.

"After one week of being in the hospital, the doctors diagnosed you with having polio. I was scared. In those days, a polio diagnosis meant that sooner or later the child was going to die. Having to give attention to your two sisters kept me sane. After the girls would be placed in bed for the night, I lay crying. Not only did I have to deal with the fact that my only son was going to die, the man I had completely given my life to was getting his comfort from the arms of another woman. Guilt consumed me and I felt overwhelmed and oh so alone. For the first time I had to leave my children with a baby sitter. Your sisters cried everyday, day in and day out. The stress of either finding a job soon or losing the house and being thrown out to the street with my three very young children drained my faith. I'd pray and just didn't feel God in my hour of need. I could not be comforted. I knew it was just a matter of time before I got the dreaded call. The call came sooner than I thought.

"In less than a month's time, the polio had run its destructive course. Early one morning I got the call. 'Mrs. Pantages, please come quickly. Your son is dying.' I felt as if time stood still. Your grandma came to the house to take care of the girls so I could rush to the hospital. There in the children's ward, I saw lots of other children sick with polio as well. While visiting you, I met other parents who had lost their children to this horrific disease. I was haunted by the remembrance of their agony, heartache, and the anguish they demonstrated as they watched the nurses roll their dead children towards the morgue.

"Within me I shouted, 'No! God, You can not let my child die. You promised in Your prophecy to me that my son would live.' Guilt of the fact that I had not been faithful in serving the Lord lessened my hope of calling out to God. I questioned myself. 'How could He hear me? Why would He want to perform a miracle for a woman who had forgotten Him?' With every bit of strength and hope, I had to take a chance and prayed out to God one more time. 'Lord you know that I have not been faithful the way I should have. I'm coming to You today, not for me, but for my little boy. I know that I really don't deserve anything from You, but I just want to remind You that we presented him to You and he belongs to You. I'm not asking You to heal him for me, but I am asking You to heal him because he is Your son.

I remember my mom crying as she reminisced her prayer. I reached out to hold her hands and she continued.

"After I prayed, I still remember how a beautiful feeling of peace fell upon me. For the first time in a very long time, I honestly felt God had heard my prayer. I called the pastor, who immediately came. He prayed a short but powerful prayer of faith and called upon the name of Jesus, as he anointed your little head with oil. You were miraculously healed. Your grandfather's words of prophecy had been fulfilled."

Peace and Understanding

Peace and understanding. Understanding and peace. They seem to go together very much the same way that salt and pepper, peanut butter and jelly, and Lucy and Ethel do. They are inseparable; at least that is what I thought when I read Philippians 4:7 in the King James Version. For years and years, I thought that the peace of God would pass on to me all understanding, and once understanding came, it would keep my heart and mind through Christ Jesus. Little did I know that this was not true on both counts.

Do you remember as a child breaking your head trying to figure out math problems? Weren't you taught, as I was, to believe that for every problem there was a solution? Then, once it was figured out, wasn't there a great sense of accomplishment that would materialize, and the hope that the next problem could be tackled more easily? As students in school, weren't we taught if the solution could not be found, it only meant a better effort was needed, which subsequently pointed back to the drawing board?

Hasn't the need to find understanding been part of our human nature? Isn't being able to understand a form of gaining knowledge? Isn't there usually a sense of satisfaction and contentment when understanding is achieved? Does the feeling of satisfaction and contentment guarantee the feeling of peace? Perhaps not. To this day, my children honestly believe that algebraic equations are sent from the pit of hell and that there are no solutions to these devilishly-inspired problems; then again that's another story.

Not only is the peace of God better than understanding (the New King James Version uses *surpasses* instead of *passes*), I discovered that understanding a situation doesn't always bring peace. Let me explain. There may be times living as Christians that the non-converted people we come in contact with just don't like us.

They appear to dislike everything about the way we walk, the way we talk, and even the way we handle situations. Why? Because a true Christian will live the life they supposedly say is impossible to live, and the weaknesses of unbelievers are exposed. I say this not condescendingly, but from my own personal experience before I came to know the Lord. Without saying a word, the Christian life speaks volumes, and at times speaks so loudly that an unconverted person cannot bear the fact that their life has been found wanting.

When God was dealing with me to accept His salvation, He would use the lives of Christian people as examples, showing me that it was possible to live in a Godly way. To shift the guilt away from my corner to theirs, I would begin to nitpick, find fault, and lie. Now when others do the same to me and the understanding of these encounters comes to my knowledge, peace is not the first characteristic that comes to heart. If anything, anxiety sets in and I begin to wonder what can be done to remedy the problem, if at all possible. It is known through Scripture that,

> *If it is possible, as much as depends on you, live peaceably with all men*
>
> Romans 12:18

That's easier said than done, and now the face of God must be sought for wisdom to help in a situation that we did not bring upon ourselves.

Just One Word

To illustrate this point further, let me recount a situation that happened in our local church. Our pastor had been sick for some time, and finally getting him to go to the doctor was a miracle in and of itself. We as the congregation felt that if he could get help for his sickened body, then the church could continue working on winning souls for the kingdom of God. He went in to take some tests; the results of which took a couple of weeks. When he finally announced the results, never will I forget the reaction of the entire congregation with the uttering of just one word. CANCER! There were looks of disbelief while others shed tears. Hearing the word alone sent our minds racing with thousands of unanswered questions. Did we hear him right? Surely there was a mistake. CANCER? It can't be! He's too young. Understanding the situation that day did not bring peace. If anything, knowing what was wrong caused more turmoil in the congregation than I had ever seen. We were expecting to leave this meeting with our minds at ease, yet understanding the situation only paralyzed us with fear.

This is why Jesus offers His children something better than understanding, whether one can grasp difficult times or not. He said,

Peace I leave with you, My peace I give to you; not as the world gives do I give to you. Let not your heart be troubled, neither let it be afraid.

John 14:27

What is so different about this peace that Jesus offers? Well, the peace that is offered by the world in which we live is only offered when everything is going good and everyone is in agreement. On the other hand, Jesus offers a peace when life doesn't make sense, when it has turned its back on you, when we just don't understand. Ever felt you've gotten the short end of the stick? No problem. The peace of Christ is powerful enough to see you through these trying times.

I Just Don't Understand

Jairus (Luke 8:41-56) was put in a situation that no parent would ever want to have to deal with: his only daughter was dying. He approached Jesus with the hope that He would come to his house to heal her. Jairus knew that they must hurry, because his daughter lay dying, and any delay would be detrimental. But as they journeyed to Jairus' house, they encountered a throng of people trying to get the Lord's attention. Fighting their way through this great multitude, Jairus did his best to get Jesus to his house on time. The people though, not knowing the situation and having their own problems that they needed Jesus to deal with, were not about to let go of perhaps the only opportunity they would ever have to receive their miracle. It is at this point that the story of Jairus is put on the shelf, and the Biblical author continues with yet another woman who is in distress.

This woman has an issue of blood (ie, hemorrhage), which had cost her her life savings. No doctor in the land had been able to find a cure for her, and she, too, was dying. In desperation, it had come down to either she received an answer from Jesus that day or she would die. She made a decision that, come what may, she would pursue Jesus to get her healing.

No Guarantees

Making a decision to touch God does not guarantee that this answer will come easily. It never does. Picture, if you will, a blue light special at Kmart, with people fighting for that last item on sale. Multiply that by one thousand both in number and intensity. Then you will better understand what this woman was coming up against as she inched slowly toward the Master. Being punched, kicked, cursed at, grabbed, and knocked to the floor, it was still not enough to deter her. She believed that if she could just touch the hem of His garment, she would be healed (Luke 8:44). She felt that she didn't need to talk to Him or look Him face to face. She didn't even need to get His attention just one touch of His garment would be enough to do what no doctor could do, and that was to heal her sickened body.

What speaks to me more about this woman than anything else is the fact that when she touched His garment she was on her knees. There is something about humbling oneself in the presence of God that will always catch His attention. It was with this touch that Jesus stopped and asked the question, "Who touched me?" Even Peter was baffled by this question, noting that hundreds, maybe thousands, had been touching Him now for a period of time (Luke 8:45). But it was just one touch, not grabbing, or pulling, or yanking, or tugging that caused virtue to flow from Him. It was just one simple touch from a woman completely humbled, brought to her knees.

That's the way it is when you come into the presence of God. Those that go there frequently know what I'm talking about. There is a calm assurance that if I can just touch Him today, I know that everything is going to be all right.

As the woman answered His question, Jesus was amazed by her faith and let her know that this faith is what made her whole (Luke 8:47-48). Both Jesus and this woman knew that her touching a man was out of order, even more so for a woman whose disease was rendered as unclean. It was not only appalling and inappropriate, but was completely unlawful. She

16

took the greatest of risks, with no guarantee that Jesus would honor her faith.

Jesus doesn't necessarily always respond to need, but He will always respond to faith. After Jesus' declaration, the crowd was aroused by the great miracle that they had witnessed, and they showed their approval with shouts of glory to God.

But where's Jairus in all of this? Could it be that, as happy as he was that this woman had received her healing, he still understood that if Jesus didn't arrive in time, his daughter was going to die? Perhaps he thought, "What about me, Jesus, you're taking too long. What about my daughter who is dying?" Have you ever felt that way, believing the Lord is taking too long to respond to your petition? Have you ever participated in a power-packed, Holy Ghost filled service where the glory of God is falling upon everyone else except you? You have been waiting on God now for a period of time. You have been as patient as you possibly can be. You have a promise from God that He's going to come to the rescue, but if He doesn't hurry, the request might die. "What about me Jesus, have you forgotten about me?" Yes, we do know what Jairus was going through!

After getting through the multitude of people, the journey finally began again, and Jairus began to calm down. Just as he had become comfortable, believing that Jesus would still get to his house on time, he received news of his daughter's death (Luke 8:49). "What do you mean she's dead? There's got to be a mistake. That can't be, because I have a promise from God. If this is really true, I just don't understand."

When Jesus looked Jairus straight in the eye and uttered these simple words, it sounded as if He was speaking in another language, "Do not be afraid, only believe" (Luke 8:50). The fact of the matter was, he was afraid. How could he believe Jesus when He had just broken His promise to come heal his daughter? None of this made sense. He so badly wanted to believe the words of the Master, but his heart was telling him otherwise. His mind could have easily taken him back to all the times that he and his daughter shared together. No one really knows for sure what he was thinking, but as a father myself, he may have been remembering pushing her on the swings, chasing her like a big ugly monster trying to scare her half to death, teaching her how to ride her bike, and picking her up every time she fell when she was just learning how to skate. On and on go the memories. How could he possibly live without her? As his mind continued to race out of control, out of nowhere a sense of peace began to rise in his heart. Without any understanding at all, he started to believe Jesus for the impossible.

Moving Into the Supernatural

As they arrived at the home of Jairus, they were greeted by the wails of the lamenters that had been hired (a Jewish custom) to mourn the death of his daughter. "Do not weep; she is not dead, but sleeping" (Luke 8:52). The ridicule of Jesus' words by these lamenters (Luke 8:53) was partly due to their unbelief, but also knowing that if it was true, they were out of a job. What comes next is something that everyone should apply to our lives when we are to believe God for a miracle. He kindly dismissed all of those that did not believe. Now He could move on into the supernatural without the opposition that unbelief always carries with it, and He raised her from the dead. As Jairus hugged his daughter as only a father can, I'm sure that he was glad that he did not allow his emotions to dictate what Jesus was going to do. His obedience to the promise of God brought life, as it always will.

Peace, Be Still

I could go on and on with other examples of how God provides without us having to understand the situation completely. But in reality, there's something inside of us that "just has to understand," and it always throws us for a loss. It's exactly what the disciples felt when the storm was raging on the Sea of Galilee and Jesus was asleep below (Mark 4:35-41).

There was no explanation as to why they were going to die that day. All of the signs pointed to drowning at sea, and as far as they were concerned, Jesus didn't even care. When they finally woke Him up, they were appalled over the fact that He was so calm. Maybe He didn't understand the situation, they thought, and needed some help making things clear. Or maybe He's in over His head and just doesn't want to admit it. For all the questions that were going around and around in their heads, there's one thing that Jesus did not do. He did not give them an explanation. Without a word, He confidently moved to the front of the boat and uttered three words that they will never forget. "Peace, be still" (Mark 4:39). What He was really doing was offering them something better than understanding, His peace. Will peace always take away the storms of life? Will He always come in the nick of time to help us evade the painful moments life brings? I can answer those questions with one big emphatic NO! But on the other hand, the peace that He offers is far superior than anything understanding could bring to our lives. If one could only trust God's purpose in dealing with His children in this manner we wouldn't be such crybabies. Why is it that when the difficult times of life come our way, our prayers to the Father are those of total despair? Like the disciples, we feel as if our life is coming to an end and we are about to perish. But God in His wisdom allows these difficult times to come for two reasons. First off, trying times will many times draw us closer to Him. When we have hit rock bottom, it is somewhat easier to look up to Him. Yet most important is the fact that, as we struggle through the storms of life, there are others, who do not know the Lord, that are watching us. They do not care what our lives are like when everything is going good. They want to find answers as to how one gets through what feels like the impossible when everything is falling apart. When we are faithful to God even in the most difficult of times, our lives speak louder to them than any amount of witnessing that we could do. Knowing that your heart is about to break because of marital problems, or the fact that your child has just run away, how can you still be smiling after all that? They will flat out ask, "What in the world is your secret?" Your answer to them will simply be, "Jesus." You could go on like the rest of the Christian world, asking God to take away the pain, the tragedy, the loss, the heart break, but you would be forfeiting one of the greatest gifts God has to offer us. That gift is His peace in the midst of a storm.

A Lesson Learned

I no longer waste time in the presence of God asking for answers to situations that I do not understand. I have gleaned so much from my mom's example that it makes it almost impossible to do so. I was miraculously healed, we never lost the house, and my mom found a good paying job. But the most important thing that happened in our family was my mom found her way back to God.

I've known Him now long enough to trust that when I don't understand the hard times in life, somewhere down the line He's going to make it right. And although understanding the situation would be nice, I have also learned that *"the peace of God, which surpasses all understanding,"* shall keep my heart and mind through Christ Jesus (Phil. 4:7).

Chapter 2
Just Do It

His mother said to the servants, "Whatever He says to you, [just] do it."

John 2:5

Giving orders today is not as simple and clear-cut as in the past. Nowadays, orders are usually followed by a one word question. What would that word be? "Why," of course! It's not enough to just do as one is told, there has to be an explanation that comes with it. If the explanation is not clear enough, or if it doesn't make any sense, we are then challenged to change the order, or at least allow it to be done at a later time. I remember when I was growing up in the 1960s, Grandma or Grandpa would give an order, and whether I understood it or not, I obeyed. They did not want my opinion, neither did they care what I thought; in their eyes my job was to obey. Even if I looked at them wrong, they would not think twice to use Grandpa's barber belt hanging in the restroom on my back side. Boy, have things changed!

Talking about change, it's amazing how the trends of society have crept into the church. So much so that it has become difficult for a believer to obtain the mind of Christ. Whereas Christ teaches believers to deny themselves in following Him, many Christians today are so "rights"-oriented that even God is questioned when He tries to set lives in order. There are issues and reservations many have that obstruct the will of God from being done. Why? They are obstructed because, if our orders don't make sense and we don't understand the situation completely, then we are not in agreement. That disagreement yields to disobedience, which in turn denies the blessing of God. The problem is this: there are occasions that God chooses not to explain things. We must then be able to trust that He knows what He's doing and has our best interests in mind. With God, timing is everything, and if He is to be delayed by our constantly questioning Him (lack of faith), then many times the will of God will pass on by.

Setting the Stage

To fully understand the scripture mentioned at the beginning of this chapter (John 2:5), I need to take some time to explain how orders were given and received in the times that Jesus lived. First of all, only those in authority could give orders. If a peer was giving the orders, it didn't need to be obeyed. Secondly, once an order was given, change could only come from the person who first gave it. For example, if you had more than one boss and received orders that morning from one boss to dig ditches the rest of the day, while another boss at noontime came and asked you to go golfing with him, you couldn't because you were bound to the first order. Finally, disobeying an order was not taken as lightly as it is today. If a subordinate chose to disobey an order, the punishment could be anything from being fired to being taken out of the city and stoned to death. Now let me take some time to reflect on Mary, the mother of Jesus. She is found at a wedding in Cana of Galilee, and, for what ever reason, she begins to give orders to the servants. This is so out of character for her, because not only was she a quiet woman (Luke 2:19, 51), women in those times did not speak in public. To make matters worse, she wasn't even part of the family, she was only an invited guest from out of town. What is the bottom line? She's out of order. Something had to have happened to trigger such outbursts. This change in character actually begins shortly after the baptism of her son Jesus.

For the first time in thirty years, Mary will not be considered that crazy woman from Nazareth. What do you mean your son is the Messiah? You see, now that Jesus had started His ministry, the rest of the world would know what she had harbored in her heart from the time the angel came to her and explained that the child in her womb would be the long-awaited Messiah.

It amuses me to hear people say that as Christians we use God as a crutch, when in reality what must be endured is far more difficult than for any nonbeliever. God has never sheltered His children from the painful experiences of life. He does, though, supply whatever is needed to come out victorious. Included comes the ability to turn the other cheek, accept responsibility when it's not your fault, and probably the most difficult of all, stay quiet when it would be easy to defend yourself. Most people don't realize what Mary had to give up in becoming the mother of the Christ child. Every young lady dreams of the day that she will walk down the aisle with all eyes glued upon her because it is her wedding day. Saying yes to Jesus meant that she would have to forfeit the most exciting day in her personal life. All of the glitter and glamour would be replaced by rumor, lies, and the scandal of a pregnancy out of wedlock. To add insult to injury, they would have to escape to another city so that her baby could be born in safety and could not return until things had died down. Watching her son being rejected throughout His entire ministry was to be commonplace, culminated by enduring His death on the cross. But at that moment, it really didn't matter. All that she could think about was what was about to happen in the lives of those who would come in contact with Jesus. Old Testament Scripture (Isa. 61:1, Ps. 72:13) in particular would confirm what she always knew in her heart. The blind would see, the lame would walk, lepers would be cleansed, the deaf would hear, the dead would be raised, and the Gospel would be preached to the poor (Luke 4:18, 19).

If in the eyes of others she was out of order because of her outburst at the wedding, then so be it, but she was willing to stir the waters so that the will of God could be done.

<u>Making Waves</u>

"Just doing it" will always make waves. When a pastor friend of mine took on the challenge of his first pastorate, one of the first things that he began to teach the congregation was the importance of worship. One Sunday morning as the congregation was in one mind and in one accord, their praises went up as God's blessings came down. As the intensity of their worship continued to grow, a pregnant woman walked in completely lost and in total despair. As she walked down the aisle moaning and groaning, it was easy to see that she needed help. Instead of having the ushers escort her out of the sanctuary to be dealt with on a one-on-one basis, the pastor stopped the service and decided to deal with her himself. She excused herself from the pastor, not realizing that she had walked into a church.

"I'm sorry for disturbing you, but I just returned from the hospital with bad news. The baby in my womb has died and I really don't know what to do because they cannot operate for another couple of days. I'm going crazy because it was the little girl that I have always wanted and now they are telling me she's dead."

As the pastor was waiting for God to give him the wisdom to handle this situation accordingly, he immediately rejected the first thought that came to mind. Through His Spirit, the Lord said, "I want you to choose the lady that has caused the most trouble in the church to come up to the altar so that she can pray for this woman, and I will resurrect the baby."

"You mean that long-tongued, short-fused, out-of-control woman that almost caused a split in the church?" objected the pastor.

"That's the one," responded the Lord.

"But God she's . . ."

"Just do it."

Knowing that continuing this discussion would not change God's mind, he called the lady up to the altar area. Now when this unfaithful member heard what the pastor was requesting, she believed that others had told him the gossip that she had been spreading against him. According to her, the only reason he wanted her to come up was so that he could embarrass her in front of the entire congregation and even things up. As she was about ready to get up and leave the sanctuary, she heard the voice of God say, "Just do it." With a great deal of apprehension, she decided to obey the voice of God and make her way up. With the help of six other women, she laid her hand on the stomach of this pregnant woman and began to pray. The congregation began to get a burden for this woman, and together they prayed for the power of God upon the lifeless child. Immediately, the baby began to kick inside the womb. The mother became hysterical, shouting, "My baby's alive; she's kicking me so hard. I can't believe it, she's really alive." When the congregation heard her declaration, their intensity of worship increased to the point that the entire place was shaken by the glory of God. The best part of this testimony was not only did that woman receive her miracle that day, she also received the baptism of the Holy Ghost and was saved. What happened to that gossiping lady that was always causing problems? She became a great soul winner like that church had never seen before. "Just doing it" sometimes has great benefits that don't make themselves available unless we take a step of faith.

Jesus Gets Into the Act

Returning back to St. John chapter two, we observe that Jesus was now getting into the act of giving orders. He instructed the servants to fill the water pots and transport them to the head table. Notice that He didn't say "Refill the water pots." Water pots were always put at the entrance of the dining hall, with the purpose of cleansing those that had come in off of the dirty street. They weighed between 150 to 200 pounds, and, by tradition, were not to be moved for any reason. Refilling them to the brim meant that they were mixing dirty water with clean water. The end result would be to serve dirty water to the head table. The servants had a great decision to make. They understood the laws of the day and how orders could not be changed by anyone other than the one who had given them. But there was something about the way this man, Jesus, spoke. They had never seen Him before, they didn't know who He was, and He was requesting something that was completely out of order. Yet His words were convincing enough that they were willing to take a chance of not only losing their jobs, but perhaps losing their lives. To "just do it" is when one is willing to sacrifice everything, denying one's own wishes, even if it means to go against tradition and obey the command.

I was in Georgia a couple of years back, ministering in a church for the first time. Seeing the gifts of the Spirit move so freely was a new experience for them, and every move that I made was carefully watched. As I began to deal with a man who was in church for the first time, the Lord revealed to me that he had back problems. Before I laid hands on him, the word of knowledge began to reveal other things about his life. I said, "Sir, although you're here in line to be healed, that's not the real reason why you came church." I continued saying, "Before you came to church tonight, your wife kicked you out of the house because she was fed up with your drug and alcohol problem. Is that true?" As he looked at me like a madman shocked by the revelation of truth, since no one else in the congregation knew who he was, he was willing to admit that God was truly speaking through me about his life. In the meantime, out of the corner of my eye, a young lady was intensely watching everything that was going on. Again through a word of knowledge, for a moment my attention focused on the desires of her heart. The Lord said to me, "She is so hungry to be used by God, but feels that it will never come to pass because she's female. Come back to her later, and I will show her how wrong she is." There came a time in the service that a group of women had come up to the altar to be healed. It was at this time that the Lord instructed me to call out that same young lady. As she approached me, she was visibly shaking and trembling, obviously scared. Noting that she was somewhat shy, withdrawn, and extremely nervous, I tried to calm her down by encouraging her to follow my lead. One of the reasons she was so beside herself was because women in her local church were not allowed to pray for the sick, and this would be breaking a long-adhered-to tradition. Let me take a sidebar here and explain one of the disadvantages of being in a Hispanic Pentecostal organization. Because Latino males are by nature very chauvinistic, it hinders growth in the kingdom of God. Thank God that little by little we are making adjustments to include our women in all facets of ministry. The problem is that changes come very, very slowly.

I instructed her to stand behind the women in line, and to put her hands on the shoulders of the woman in front of her. Next, this would be her prayer, nothing more nothing less. "In the name of Jesus, be healed. Pain be gone." She then tried to wiggle out of it by giving numerous excuses, but I stopped her in her tracks and said, "Just do it." With the fear that was so evident by the trembling in her voice, she whispered the prayer. What happened next probably frightened her more than the fear that she was already experiencing. The woman in line, who before the prayer could not move her neck, was excitedly moving it back and forth with no problem.

One would think that seeing such a great miracle happening right before her eyes would cause great excitement in this timid young lady. On the contrary, she ran to me trembling even more, with a look on her face that resembled someone who had just seen a ghost. She asked, "Brother, if I continue to pray for the rest of the ladies in line, will I feel what I felt happen again?"

I said, "I don't know, what did you feel?" I asked the question because when I minister to the sick, I feel nothing whatsoever in my body. I have friends, who have been mightily used of God in the same manner, who claim they sense the various diseases in the parts of their own body where the others are feeling pain. I just wanted to know if this was what was happening with her. She said, "When I prayed for that sister, a jolt of electricity began to run through my entire body. It got more intense as it got to my arms and hands; it felt like bolts of lightning shooting out from my body."

I said, "Sister, just keep on doing it." With the confidence that was not there when she began, she continued down the line laying hands on the sick ladies, and God healed all of them. When we got to the end of the line, I asked the last woman what her need was. She said she was blind. I realized that maybe my new helper was in over her head and asked if I could take over. By this time, not only did the anointing feel so thick, as if one could slice it with a knife, but her confidence had risen to a level reflecting that nothing was going to discourage her now. She boldly stood behind the blind woman, this time repeating the prayer at the top of her lungs, and guess what? The Lord healed the blind woman right on the spot.

Culture and religion teach that a woman cannot be used of God to this to degree in the church. God says, "Just do it."

A Moment of Truth

With the focus now on bypassing culture and religion to find the will of God, it's now possible to revisit St. John chapter two. Verse eight reveals the new orders the servants have received from Jesus. The moment of truth has now come to these servants, who have totally disregarded their initial orders to obey the voice of God. The new order they hear from the Master is even more ridiculous than what they have heard from Him up to this point. "Draw out NOW."

He's asking that they serve the "dirty water" to those who are at the head table. Obeying God is always a NOW kind of thing. No time to think, no time to figure things out, no time to evaluate. We cannot question, and most definitely can't have a "come back tomorrow attitude"; it has to be done at that moment. There's no turning back; one must be able to freefall into His presence believing that what ever is about to happen, it will be for one's best. The hardest part of obeying God is that many times He waits until the last second.

It is my opinion that the water turned into wine as it was being served to the head table. Why do I feel this way? Because that's exactly how God deals in my life. Can you imagine the looks the servants were getting from the invited guests when they began to serve the dirty water? How about the anxiety they themselves felt? What in the world am I doing? Have I lost my mind? The fact of the matter is, when Jesus speaks, are we as Christians willing to chuck it all just so we can be pleasing in His sight?

A young man was sent from the United States to Africa as a first-time missionary. With so much excitement and enthusiasm, he believed that God was going to do great things in his ministry. As he began to put his entire effort into the work of God, the Lord began to bless in a great and mighty way. Entire tribes were being filled with the Holy Ghost and accepting the salvation plan. The response to the gospel allowed the Spirit to flow so freely that signs, wonders, and miracles became commonplace. Not a day passed by without something miraculous occurring that caused more and more people to come to the saving knowledge of Jesus Christ. Of course, when Satan caught wind of the great revival that was going on, it was only a matter of time before he was going to try to stop it.

For the next few weeks, a great famine made its way to that part of Africa. With complications in communicating with the United States, the missionary wasn't able to get the necessary help. The weeks turned into months, and the restlessness of the newly converted tribesmen began to show. Finally, after a few months, the tribal chief paid a visit to the missionary, declaring, "If within the next seven days your God cannot provide for us food and water, then we're going back to our old ways (cannibalism), and you will be our first meal." In the eyes of the missionary, seven days was more than sufficient time to find an answer from God. He began a major time of prayer and fasting, but to no avail. Seven days passed, there's still no answer from God. The tribal chief and his buddies made their way to visit the missionary once again. With one last prayer, the missionary finally received his orders from God. The Lord impressed him to do the unthinkable. "Take your Bible and place it in one of the ovens found in the courtyard. Wait for half an hour and then take it out.

"But God."

"Just do it."

Still not completely convinced that he had just heard from God, he continued to complain. Again the Lord simply responded with, "Just do it." He figured he didn't have anything to lose. If anything, he'd buy more time to hear the "real" orders that God would give him. So he went to the courtyard and put the Bible in the oven as he was told and waited.

He had completely forgotten where the verses in the Bible had declared several times that the Scriptures can be to us the "bread of life." Because of that loss in memory, the next half hour was an eternity. But low and behold, to their great surprise, when they finally opened the oven door, the Bible had been replaced by a loaf of bread. The missionary then collected all of the Bibles he possibly could, and for the next couple of days, continued to place them in the oven. What happened that day in the courtyard spread like wildfire, and the greatest revival that part of Africa had ever seen became history. Why did God have to wait till the last minute? He really didn't have to, but that's just His way. When God tests His children, it's not for His sake, but rather for ours. In His wisdom, He already knows the outcome when we are pressured in everyday life. On the other hand, we are the ones that must follow Him, by faith, to the end that we might truly learn that He will never leave us nor forsake us (Heb. 13: 5).

<u>Up Close and Personal</u>

The lessons that can be learned from the second chapter of John are countless and can be a blessing to anyone who is willing to apply them in their Christian walk. What I am about to write now comes from a very personal lesson taught to me from verse ten.

> *And he said to him, "Every man at the beginning sets out the good wine, and when the guests have well drunk, then the inferior. **You have kept the good wine until now!**"*
>
> John 2:10

For all the miracles that have been part of my ministry now for many years, I remember when this was not so. When I gave my heart to God back in 1972, I was nothing more than a shy,

31

withdrawn, handicapped young man that loved God. Sharing the Word in front of a crowd was nearly impossible, because whenever I spoke the tears would flow uncontrollably and no one could make out what I was trying to say. I had such a hunger for God, I was willing to do anything and everything possible just to draw closer to Him. I remember the anxiety I felt after our early morning Sunday prayers and fasting. The young men of the church would then get together to talk about sports. As much as I am a fan of the Lakers, USC football, the Dodgers, etc., I just couldn't bring myself to stand there talking sports when there was an opportunity to get closer to God. So I would excuse myself, go to my car, and, with my Bible open, begin to search the Scriptures to find God for myself. Time passed and many of those same young men were initiated to the ministry. The fact that I was included in that bunch was a miracle in and of itself. I was so far behind the rest of them in communication skills that it appeared the only reason I had been initiated was because the pastor was family. Of course, when the invitations came around to preach at youth functions, youth camps, and youth conventions, I was usually the one that was left out. These young men followed the lead of our pastor, who is a fireball of a preacher. With their dynamic messages, they easily got people on their feet shouting, running aisles, jumping, and dancing. All I could ever do was make people cry. As much as I tried to conform to our Pentecostal ways, I was really more of a Jeremiah than an Elijah. I got to the point that I honestly felt that I didn't have what it took to be a successful preacher. How could I ever believe that God would be willing to use somebody like me? So the years went on with not much success, feeling more and more depressed, until a call to pastor a church came to my life.

After thirteen years of living in obscurity, now, as a pastor, I believed that God would use me like never before. For the next seven years, I completely dedicated myself to the new church that my family and I had planted. It didn't matter to me that starting from scratch was going to be a difficult task. I remember going door to door on Saturday mornings trying to get home Bible studies started, so that people could know God. Sundays would come and I would do everything from cleaning the church, setting things up, and more. I would teach the Sunday school class, direct the song service, preach, and then work the altar until I was completely exhausted. Working a secular job at the time made things a little bit more difficult, but it didn't matter to me because I just wanted to do the will of God. All my efforts were nearly in vain because, after seven years of backbreaking work, the congregation had only grown to at most forty. Again my self esteem began to wane, because I felt that God just didn't love me. I knew that I was not cut out in the Pentecostal mold that other successful pastors were: I was too mellow for that. Nevertheless, giving everything that I had, in my mind, had to count for something. I took a great leap of faith to lease a building big enough to help run a day-care center. After six months of toiling in this new venture, there were not enough children enrolled to help us make ends meet financially. Because the congregation was still very small, we could not make up the difference in helping to pay the bills. One day, my wife, who also worked in the day care, left that part of the building to go to the sanctuary during lunchtime. There she would kneel before the presence of God completely broken, pleading that He would give her husband the wisdom, courage, and the answers needed to make this thing work. She would return back to work with her eyes red and swollen, believing that God was going to give her an answer. She would at times tell me why her prayers were so emotional and what she was feeling. It would only put more pressure on me to find the answers I was looking for. When God did speak to me regarding the future of our church and how He was going to make it grow, in my eyes it appeared too simplistic. Isn't that just how God is? He brings our answers to the lowest degree, so that even in our confusion we can figure things out.

*But God has chosen the foolish things of the world to put
to shame the wise, and God has chosen the weak things
of the world to put to shame the things which are mighty;
and the base things of the world and the things which are
despised God has chosen, and the things which are not, to
bring to nothing the things that are,* **that no flesh
should glory in His presence.**

1 Corinthians 1:27-29

So what then is the problem? Our flesh gets in the way,
won't allow us to accept God's answer, and we lose out on His
will. That is exactly what happened to me: my flesh overrode
the wisdom of God, and, in time from my frustration, I turned
in the church to our Bishop. Little did I know that my decision
would cause a downward spiral spiritually that would take years
to repair. Leaving the pastorate meant that I would have to find
a secular job, look for a new house, find a new local church,
and deal with the fallout of having to explain why the church
failed not to mention the effect that this was going to have on
my wife and family.

Gradually, bitterness set in. Being no respecter of persons,
it crept into every member of the family. My wife felt so
humiliated that she no longer wanted to attend church, feeling
that God had not answered her plea, so what's the use? Feeling
her hurt did nothing for my self-esteem. Already fighting the
thoughts that God did not love me, having to deal with her
depressions was only adding fuel to the fire. I had made up my
mind that although I would not completely turn my back on
God, neither would I take great steps of faith as I had in the
past, making myself vulnerable to failure. Those thoughts
sounded so good racing through my mind, if only they would
have been acceptable to my heart.

As I accepted an invitation to visit a particular local
church, my intentions were only to put on a good show
outwardly guarding my broken heart. Months had passed since
God had spoken to me; yet when He did in that service, I knew

it was Him. "I would like to make you a deal," He said. "I will restore everything that you have lost, including your wife's love for Me. All I ask of you is this one thing. Every time you walk into My house, I want you to worship Me with everything you have, holding nothing back." Although at that time it was going to take some effort to comply with the Lord's wishes, I felt that it was doable, and I was willing to take that chance. Within a matter of weeks we had a new home; I got a new job; we found a new church; and my wife was miraculously changed, giving herself completely onto the Lord.

Ministry wasn't part of the original deal, and I was thankful for that, because I really didn't want to minister again. With all that I had suffered through my entire life, and with all of my shortcomings, I just felt that it was best to leave that part of my life under the rubble of my failed pastorate. Of course, God had other plans. For the first time in over ten years, a prophet of God from Virginia accepted an invitation to come to California. It just so happened that one of the churches that he was going to speak to was in our area. A number of us got together, hoping and praying that this man of God would call us out and minister to us individually. The meeting was more than five hours, and, as he continued to minister to hundreds of people one-on-one, about halfway into the service, the Lord told me not to worry. He assured me that I would be the last one that the man of God would minister to that evening. Sure enough, it happened exactly as God said it would.

We invited the prophet to lunch the next day, and he graciously accepted. Trying to eat and ask questions at the same time proved to be quite a task. Sensing our hunger for the things of God, he began to minister unto us. Again I was one of the last ones to hear a direct word from God. The words that I was about to hear were going to be ones that would change the course of the rest of my life. He said, "Son, living for God has been very, very difficult for you. No matter what you have done, or how hard you have tried, it's been like bumping your head against a brick wall. Your frustrations have been so great that you have pretty much quit trying to live a life of faith. God wanted you to know that your success in the things of God have not been held back because God doesn't love you. Neither have they been held back because God has not protected you from the onslaught of the devil. It was God in His wisdom who was holding back blessing because *He was saving your best for last.*"(John 2:10) I finally realized that for years I was just ahead of my time. The heartfelt messages that God had given me during this time were ones that this lost world was still not prepared to receive. Dealing with major disappointments, losses, and heartbreak would only groom me for such a time as this. To think that all this time all God was trying to do was to prepare me for the next level, instead of trying to destroy me as I had so foolishly thought. It not only makes me feel so unworthy of the kindness that He has shown, but it also makes me feel more indebted in His service.

"Just do it." It is such a simple concept that we find at the very core of every successful man or woman of God. Choices, adjustments, and sacrifices become part of their everyday life. In my case, I had to say "YES" to a major change in my ministry. Until I was willing to make that change, everything that had been prophesied over me would be put on hold.

Chapter 3
When I Said Yes

Also I heard the voice of the Lord, saying: "Whom shall I send, And who will go for Us?" Then I said, "Here am I! Send me."

Isaiah 6:8

Responding to the call of God is easier said than done. The feeling of inadequacy is usually strong enough to keep us away from the perfect will of God. Why? I think that because in our eyes we are never good enough to be used by Him. What adds even more anxiety to accepting the call of God is that what He is asking of us usually will stretch our faith to the max. Not being in control, venturing out into the unknown, and usually doing it alone are not the best ingredients for success. So we take our time in assessing the situation, hoping that maybe if we wait long enough God will just go away and find somebody else. If we are truly sensitive to the Spirit of the Lord, we will eventually come around and say yes. The problem is this: knowing that timing with God is everything, if we wait too long, the will of God will pass us by.

> *For many are called, but few are chosen.*
> Matthew 22:14

Misinterpreting God's Criteria

Then when He actually does choose someone else, we are offended. We moan and grown over the fact that we have been passed over for someone better. That's when the pity party begins. We misinterpret God's criteria for being used and come to the conclusion that we will never be the one that is chosen by God. Because we do not fall into the category of the perfect, we begin to believe that God will always look elsewhere. What we fail to realize is that God rarely uses people that are perfect. He rather searches for those that will make themselves totally available to Him. He seeks out those that will not gripe or complain, but grasp that His call is the greatest thing that they could ever respond to. His desires become their desires, and, when seeking God, it becomes more of a pleasure than drudgery. Our spirit is completely in tune with His spirit, in one mind and in one accord. There are no disagreements, disappointments, or disillusionments; all is done to the glory of God.

> *You will show me the path of life; In Your presence is fullness of joy; At Your right hand are pleasures forevermore.*
> Psalm 16:11

Ah! Experiencing the fullness of joy when we enter into His presence is something that we never get tired of, because when we are at His side, His pleasures extend out through eternity. So why then do most of us as Christians live in misery, unfulfilled in God? Could it be that, as the call of God comes to our life, we are saying yes with conditions? We want to do the will of God, but on our terms, at our time, at our convenience. How soon have we forgotten that we have been ". . . *bought with a price: therefore glorify God in your body, and in your spirit, which are God's*" (1 Cor. 6:20). We don't have a right to pick and choose as we please, because we no longer belong to ourselves. Jesus paid the price on Calvary and we belong to Him.

Jeremiah's Call

When the call of God came upon the prophet Jeremiah, he was still in his mother's womb. God wanted him even before he was born, because He knew what could be done with a man that would say yes without reservation. Responding to God was not as easy for Jeremiah as most would think. As he grew older, his insecurities grew more and more, and to overcome them would be quite a challenge. He was not only young, inexperienced, and hopelessly unprepared, but adding the office of a prophet to his priesthood was quite a stretch. Look how God had to encourage him at a time when his fears almost caused him to back out.

> "*Do not be afraid of their faces, For I am with you to deliver you,*" *says the LORD. Then the LORD put forth His hand and touched my mouth, and the LORD said to me: "Behold, I have put My words in your mouth."*
> Jeremiah 1:8-9

The key to this whole encounter with God is when the Lord stretches forth His hand and touches his mouth. For a person that has the gift of gab and can easily express himself in public, these Scriptures have no real significance. But to those who are somewhat shy, quiet, timid, and withdrawn, it makes all the difference in the world. It is when God touches us that, for the first time, the words flow freely from our mouth. There is no anxiety as to wondering what we are to say next. We can express ourselves in a fashion that captures the attention of others. Moreover, our confidence level rises to the roof, and we look for more opportunities to talk to others about Jesus. That's what a touch from God will do. In Jeremiah's case, he was first given words of judgment. These words would be the cornerstone of his success as a prophet, because they would demonstrate the authority of God that was placed in his hands. Because so much responsibility was given him at such a tender age, the Lord knew that words of skill would be necessary for him to carry out his assignment. These words of skill were nothing more than the Old Testament example of the gifts of the Spirit. The word of knowledge, the word of wisdom, and the word of prophecy had to be part of his everyday life, because who in their right mind was going to listen to a little boy who had no experience. Time and time again after listening to this boy prophet speak, many would leave scratching their heads, wondering how in the world a boy so young could have so much wisdom. It's pretty much the same reaction that the rulers of Israel had when Peter and John spoke before them in the fourth chapter of Acts. The rulers knew them as unlearned and ignorant men, which made it even more puzzling to hear them speak with such authority. What the rulers didn't know was that a short time ago on the day of Pentecost, God touched their mouths, and with the Holy Ghost now residing in their hearts, the right word for the right person at the right time always would be available. We can use Jeremiah as an example to help us understand how God would like to use us in a similar fashion. Like Jeremiah, we have received the authority to do some pretty amazing stuff. Look how the Lord put it to Jeremiah in chapter one, verse 10.

> *"See, I have this day set you over the nations and over the kingdoms, To root out and to pull down, To destroy and to throw down, To build and to plant."*
>
> Jeremiah 1:10

If we can accept these assignments with godly authority, applying them to our personal lives, then we will not only be able to expose the devil, stopping him in his tracks, but also be able to defeat his every purpose as we live for God. That being said, the million dollar question has to be this: why in the world are we not living as victoriously as the Scriptures have promised?

When Fear Dominates Us

The answer is found in a two-headed monster called *fear*. We not only have a tremendous fear of suffering, but we equally fear being ill-equipped. Let's take some time talking about suffering. We see suffering as nothing more than a necessary evil. It is something that we endure without ever realizing the benefits that come with it. We are so concerned about getting through it that the still small voice of God is ignored completely as we try to weasel our way out of this time of discomfort. The apostle Paul saw things so differently. All you have to do is read his account in Philippians to know that we have not yet come to his level of understanding the suffering that comes our way.

> *That I may know Him and the power of His resurrection, and the **fellowship** of His sufferings, being conformed to His death.*
> Philippians 3:10

The True Meaning of Fellowship

There is one word in that scripture that jumps out at me, that being the word *fellowship*. The apostle sees his time of suffering as nothing more than fellowship with God. When I think of fellowship, I can think of a lot of things, none of which include suffering. Fellowship to me is gathering the brethren together for a day at the park. Spending time talking, playing games, and, of course, the ultimate in fellowship, eating. Fellowship to me is a time of relaxation, a time to refresh the mind, and to enjoy others company. It is a way of recharging the batteries that have been sapped of their strength through the cares of life. Now then, if I take time to compare my definition of fellowship with that of the apostle Paul, I realize that my understanding of the word is nowhere near his. Honestly, you just don't know how much this bothered me. I had to find out why Paul saw suffering in this way and if it was the only way of seeing suffering, I needed to make an adjustment. Solomon wrote this in the book of Ecclesiastes, talking about the obtaining of knowledge, which is so true.

> *For in much wisdom is much grief, And he who*
> *increases knowledge increases sorrow.*
> Ecclesiastes 1:18

I need to clarify something before I go on. The sorrow that I feel as I increase my knowledge in the Lord is a godly sorrow. It is not one that depresses me, but one that helps me to come to great realizations in my life. The more knowledge that I receive concerning Him, the more I realize how much I really don't know, and this makes me hunger even more to know Him as He is. This godly sorrow hit me so hard when the Lord allowed me to understand why He uses suffering so frequently in our lives.

Knowing us better than we know ourselves, He allows His blessings to become sporadic in our lives, knowing that a lack of blessing will always catch our attention. When things are going good, it's so much easier to miss a day in prayer. When the bills are being paid and we are in good health, there are no good reasons to deny this flesh in fasting, so we indulge in all that we crave. On the other hand, it is when the power from on high has been shut off that our search for God becomes a little more intense. We now readily grasp the fact that God . . . *"is a rewarder of them that diligently seek him"* (Heb. 11:6 KJV). Seeking the face of God is now our number one priority, leaving no stone unturned until we find Him.

What does that say about our relationship with God? Basically that we have none until a great need arises in our life. Yet God is willing to go to those extremes, just so that He might have fellowship with us. It doesn't matter to Him that He is not our first choice. The fact of the matter is that He will take us any way He can get us. Why? Because there is hope that there may be a few out of the multitudes that come out of desperation who will continue to fellowship with Him when the problems are gone. The odds are great that few will continue this courtship with God; nevertheless, God's yearning for our fellowship is even greater.

What Strikes Even More Fear

What perhaps strikes as much fear in us as suffering is knowing that we are to go into battle ill-equipped. Like Jeremiah, we offer the same kinds of excuses as to why it's not a good idea for God to use us in the manner that He would like.

> *Then said I: "Ah, Lord GOD! Behold, I cannot speak, for I am a youth."*
>
> Jeremiah 1:6

Whether we are young, inexperienced, without formal education, or just flat out unprepared, these excuses are not sufficient turning your back on the call of God. If anything, you're exactly what God is looking for, because for great things to happen in your life would mean that God would have had to intervene for you to have any success. People would then without hesitation give God the glory for your success, which, of course, is fine with God. I have taken some time to expose the fears that hinder us from accepting the call of God. Be assured that what I have written has not come from a book or something that I heard second hand. What you are about to read is not only my personal testimony I reluctantly accepted, but a confirmation of what happens in the life of a person

43

when you respond to God's call with a weak, halfhearted, doubt-filled, "YES."

The Shock of My Life

When the call came that God wanted to change my ministry from a pastor to that of an evangelist, I responded to Him very similarly to Abraham and Sarah, when they were told that they were to give birth to a child at such an advanced age. I laughed and was amused, because I just didn't fit the Pentecostal mold of a fiery, flamboyant, in-your-face kind of preacher. Spirit-filled evangelists have the ability to move people in ways that local pastors usually can't. With dynamic, colorful, loud, and flashy messages, they make their way into the hearts of people in a way that is more than remarkable. It has been through the ministry of an evangelist that landmark changes have come to my life, when I desperately wanted to know God in a more intimate way. Taking into account how powerfully affected I had been through this type of ministry, I knew without a shadow of a doubt that I was neither prepared nor equipped to take on this new responsibility. Besides, God had given me the heart of the pastor, not that of an evangelist. If this great change in direction was going to fly, He was going to have to change my heart and equip me in ways that would make this a fair fight.

The more I pondered deeply the request that God was making (He never demands), the more frightened I became. My defense mechanisms began to kick in with the abundance of excuses taking wings. Down the line I went with an array of excuses that I thought would disqualify me immediately. But with every excuse that I offered, God calmly responded with an answer that reinforced His desire to use me anyways. When I told Him that my command of the Spanish language (90% of our churches speak Spanish only) wasn't good enough, He abruptly responded with only one word: "LEARN." When I told Him that eloquence in speaking wasn't my forte and that my messages were very basic, it fell on a deaf ear, as if He just didn't want to hear it. He then simply responded with, "You don't have to change a thing."

Little by little it began to sink in why God was so persistent in His pursuit of me. First of all, as God was making His pitch, at that time there were only three other full-time evangelists in our entire organization. The office of an evangelist had been pushed to the side almost completely to a point of extinction. Someone had to respond to the call, but as God searched throughout our ranks, He found no takers. It was those that had great bilingual preaching abilities and charismatic personalities that were turning down our Lord's offer.

The office of the pastor was more appealing, prestigious, stable, and more lucrative. The office of an evangelist in our organization was nothing more than an afterthought and didn't even come close.

Thankfully, rejection is not something that the Lord takes personally. What was happening here was very similar to the account that we find in Luke 14:16-23. In a nutshell, an invitation had been made to a feast. Those that have been invited had made excuses as to why they could not come. Notice what happens next in verse 21.

> So that servant came and reported these things to his master. Then the master of the house, being angry, said to his servant, "Go out quickly into the streets and lanes of the city, and bring in here the poor and the maimed and the lame and the blind."
>
> Luke 14:21

That's exactly where I was when Jesus came knocking at my door. Physically, the aftereffects of polio had left me lame. You should see the looks that I get as I walk down the streets in a short sleeve shirt. With my withered right arm exposed to the public, the stares that come my way aren't even subtle. Behind the pulpit, people put up with my awkward movements and my less than perfect appearance. If it weren't for the powerful anointing that has fallen upon me, most people wouldn't give me the time of day. I really didn't have a right to receive the invitation that God had extended to me. But because others that were more worthy, more qualified, and better equipped refused that same invitation, I was given the opportunity of a lifetime. Little did I know that one simple "YES" would change my life in ways that I never thought were possible.

As I undertook my new mission, I was petrified to say the least. Having to preach an entire message in Spanish and trying to beef up my messages with more of a rah-rah style made for a lot of sleepless nights. Up to this point, in almost twenty years of ministry, rarely did something out of the ordinary happen. Every once in awhile somebody would get healed or receive the baptism of the Holy Ghost, but, in all honesty, it never happened on a grand scale. However, when I said "YES," my ministry took an abrupt 180° turn.

The Turnaround Begins

I so much identified with the prophet Jeremiah in chapter 1 verse 10, when God helped him to know where he stood in His kingdom. God added to my ministry a ministry of deliverance, one that would help to root out, pull down, destroy, and throw down the devil's schemes. He then equipped me with the gifts of the Spirit. The word of knowledge began to reveal to me the problems, sicknesses, and basically the hidden things of those that I was ministering to. Of course, it was the word of wisdom that would help me to apply the knowledge that I had obtained in a fashion that would be pleasing onto God. The Lord continued blessing me with a ministry of encouragement.

Like Jeremiah, these ministries helped me to plant and build the lives of those that had been destroyed by the wiles of the devil. If that wasn't enough, God then added words of prophecy and the working of miracles. It was then that I felt that God could not possibly add anything more to my ministry than what I had already received.

Like Gomer Pyle used to say in a 1960's sitcom, "Surprise, Surprise, Surprise!" I had forgotten about a desire that I had put before the Lord as a child. Even so, God knows how to bring back those desires to the surface so that He can deal with them accordingly with the promises of His Word.

> *Delight yourself also in the LORD, And He shall give*
> *you the desires of your heart*
>
> Psalms 37:4

God knows that delighting myself in Him has always been a priority. So when my long-forgotten desire was brought back to my memory, I had no reservations making my request. The healing of my body had such a profound, lasting effect on me that I told God this: "If I could ever be used in Your kingdom, please let me lay my hands on the sick so You could heal them." To this day, and I am talking about over forty-five years ago, the vision of my healing is still very fresh in my mind. Whether it actually happened this way or not, I do not know, but this is the way that I see it.

He Walked in Looking for Me

As I mentioned in Chapter 1, my mom's heartfelt prayer was made unto God. She began to plead in the name of Jesus for her little boy's life, specifically mentioning my name. As Jesus made His way into General hospital in Los Angeles, He entered the quarantine area that housed all of us with polio. Above each doorway was a red light that flickered when death was near. It's a long corridor with dingy, green walls, and on this day many lights were flickering. Jesus began His search on the opposite side of where I was. It is beyond me how He bypassed the rest of the children that were dying. He began to poke His head inside of each room asking, "George Pantages, are you here?" When He read the name on the chart, He realized that it was not me and He continued on. So many children, so many dying, yet Jesus was only responding to one

47

woman's prayer of faith. If there was ever a lesson to be learned here, it is this: GOD ALWAYSRESPONDS TO FAITH, NOT NEED. That is the answer to the question of why it is that someone coming in off of the street with no knowledge of God can be miraculously healed when at the same time a faithful saint with a worse condition, suffering for years, is bypassed by God. Faith, faith, faith! God always responds to faith. Finally, Jesus made His way into my room. For a moment He gazed at the iron lung that was artificially giving me the breath of life, then checked the chart to make sure that the name that He was reading was the same name that my mama whispered in His presence. With just one touch of the Master's hand, His virtue flowing into my weakened little body, I was miraculously healed. Later, as the doctors gathered together to explain to my mother the great change of events (they had earlier told her that I was going to die), they sheepishly admitted that they had nothing to do with my getting better. In actuality, one doctor told my mom that whatever God she was praying to was really the one responsible for my healing. With that being said, the Lord finally added gifts of healing. I was so amazed, because at various times with simple faith God has responded with miraculous healings. As the gift began to be perfected, the healings grew not only in number but in intensity. The Lord has opened blinded eyes and He has unstopped deaf ears. In his name I have seen people healed of AIDS, leukemia (God doing blood transfusions on the spot), and cancer. Never in my wildest imaginations did I ever dream that God would use me in such astounding and wondrous ways. I had come full circle, and now life in God was mind boggling. All of the suffering that had been endured for so many years, all of the frustrations that brought with it so much confusion, all of the negative thoughts that led me to believe that God just didn't love me, was now being put all behind me. They were now to be replaced by the fruit of my labor. For all that I had gone through; I honestly believed that from this point on nothing could separate me from the love of Christ. The problem was that I had never experienced what the Bible calls an "evil day." You would think that what I had faced at one time or another had to come under that category, but it didn't. I was about to enter into the most challenging time of my Christian life, and once the dust would settle I would truly understand what an "evil day" was all about.

Chapter 4
An Evil Day

Therefore take up the whole armor of God, that you may be able to withstand in the evil day, and having done all, to stand.

Ephesians 6:13

This verse, written by the apostle Paul, is nothing more than a warning of an evil day. There are a couple of things about this scripture that stand out. First, Paul is emphatically stating an evil day is coming; no ifs, ands, or buts. Next, we must take into account that he's talking to the saved and not the unconverted. For years and years I honestly believed that this evil day could be evaded if one lived right for God. Surely only the cold in spirit and the careless were deserving of the destruction that the evil day would bring. Of course I thought I did not fall into that category; therefore I had nothing to worry about. It was for the simple reason that I had

51

completely dedicated my entire life to God in prayer and fasting. I felt totally safe, coupled with the fact that I was prepared for any battle using the whole armor of God as my protection. How could I possibly be caught unaware? It was when God began to deal with me about the above scripture that I realized that I had no clue as to what an evil day was all about.

Understanding the Evil Day

The first adjustment I had to make was the fact that the armor of God was *not* used in spiritual warfare to fight against the enemy. According to Paul it was used to withstand when an evil day came. Not expected to use the whole armor for the sole purpose of spiritual warfare goes against everything that we have been taught. So many messages and Bible studies that we have heard encourage us to pick up the "sword" and knock the snot out of the devil. To think God is asking us to step aside and just "stand" sounds so un-Christian like, if not so un-American. Just standing in the heat of the battle is not my idea of fighting. By nature, we love to fight. Since the times that we, as little kids, fought in the sandbox, to today as adults, when someone says something about our mama, we just don't back down from a fight. There are basically two reasons why it's so difficult for us to accept what the apostle is trying to teach us. First of all, there's more to "standing" than meets the eye. The literal translation means to *stand ready*. I asked myself the question, stand ready . . . for what? If God is going to do all of the fighting during this evil day, then why in the world would I need to get all dressed up in this heavy armor just to stand and do nothing? Again, doing nothing has never been God's intention for us. As I continued to inquire God for an answer, His reply was this: "When an evil day comes into your life it will be like no other. It will be a time that many will turn their backs on you. They will accuse you of things that you have not done or said. Although I will be at your side every step of the way, you will feel that your prayers are hitting the roof, only to return to the floor unanswered. My presence will be lifted and everything that you do will be by faith. Every facet of your life will be affected, and you will not know whether you are coming or going. You will walk in darkness, and even the easiest of tasks will become difficult. The fight will be taken out of you, neither having the strength nor the will to do anything about the situation. The losses will be so great that there will come a time that you will ask me to die. Remember that to me a day is as a thousand years, and there will be times that it will sure feel like it. It is for this reason that I only request one thing of my children who are suffering in this manner. You are to *"continually offer the sacrifice of praise to God."* (Heb. 13:15)

Jehoshaphat's Army Stands Still

There is an Old Testament story depicting an example of God asking His finest warriors to stand still, letting Him do all of the work. Jehoshaphat had to come to grips with these strange orders. His men were trained to fight not to stand still. However, as uneasy as this made him feel, he was sensitive enough to the voice of God to do the right thing not fight. As the time approached for God to do His thing, Jehoshaphat came up with his own crazy idea. He would trade their weapons for instruments of praise and sing praises of victory even before it had come to pass. I remember years ago our local church choir sang a popular song entitled, "Don't Wait Till The Battle Is Over, Shout Now." The song goes on to give the reason why, saying, "You know in the end we're going to win." I'm sure it wasn't the song Jehoshaphat sang that day; but you know what, it wouldn't have been a bad idea. As they began to sing their praises in the beauty of holiness, a bizarre thing took place. Without lifting a finger, the enemies of God were confounded and began to fight each other, destroying the entire army in the process. Is it any wonder that Satan fights us so hard, trying to stop the sacrifices of praise from reaching the throne of glory? He understands the power of praise and how it brings confusion into his ranks, so he goes out of his way to wreak havoc in our lives. His hopes are that in our disillusion we will keep quiet, and the power of God will not be released to defeat him again.

Once we can accept the concept of standing when an evil day comes, there is one more thing that we must take time to consider. Standing in the presence of God without our armor does us no good. The purpose of the armor is for protection, not for fighting in an actual battle. The armor can be compared to the statement that the Lord made to Satan concerning the life of Job. God said that He would allow him to do anything to Job, stopping short of taking his life (Job 1:12). That is as far as Satan can go in our lives during an evil day if we use our armor. Although it is open season on us and Satan is allowed to buffet us in whatever ways he pleases; he cannot take our life. That is the reason why putting on the armor daily is so important. The armor is our lifeline. Without it Satan can do damage that will take years to fix. Just ask King David.

A Costly Error in Judgment

To help you understand this story better, I am going to tell the story as if we were there. It was a time of war in the camp of Israel. David's men were preparing for battle and were anticipating a great victory. As they made their way through the city gates, they realized that this time their leader had decided to stay behind. David now was a greatly experienced warrior with many victories notched under his belt. In his mind, staying home this one time unarmed would not hurt him one bit. If he only knew that this decision to stay behind was going to be the moment chosen to begin an evil day, he would have done things differently. Hindsight is twenty-twenty. He went about his day being in the wrong place at the wrong time when he saw Bathsheba uncovering her body as she bathed herself.

We know the story as his lust-filled heart had her brought to the palace, committing adultery and never thinking twice about it. His sin began a downward spiral that changed the course of the rest of his life. At one time he was considered a man after God's own heart. Now, after falling during his evil day, he had become a murderer, a liar, and an adulterer, labels which would follow him to his death. Never in his wildest imaginations did he think that he could stoop that low to dishonor God. His heart was revealed as he wrote Psalm 51. Every word is drenched in agony as he struggled to find his way back into God's grace. Read it for yourself:

> *Have mercy upon me, O God, According to Your loving kindness; According to the multitude of Your tender mercies, Blot out my transgressions. Wash me thoroughly from my iniquity, And cleanse me from my sin. For I acknowledge my transgressions, And my sin is always before me. Against You, You only, have I sinned, And done this evil in Your sight That You may be found just when You speak, And blameless when You judge. Behold, I was brought forth in iniquity, And in sin my mother conceived me. Behold, You desire truth in the inward parts, And in the hidden part You will make me to know wisdom. Purge me with hyssop, and I shall be clean; Wash me, and I shall be whiter than snow. Make me hear joy and gladness, That the bones You have broken may rejoice.*
>
> Psalm 51:8

Every other word appears to be laced with remorse. Although he had sinned against Bathsheba and her husband, breaking the law in the process, his admission of guilt brought him directly before the face of God. Verse 3 confirms this when he says, *against "You [God], You only, have I sinned, and done this evil in your sight."* There is a vast difference between sinning against your brother and sinning against God. It is so much easier to dismiss our transgressions and avoid our brethren than doing so to the Master. In another portion of Scripture, he puts it this way.

> *Where can I go from Your Spirit? Or where can I flee from Your presence? If I ascend into heaven, You are there; If I make my bed in hell, behold, You are there. If I take the wings of the morning, And dwell in the uttermost parts of the sea, Even there Your hand shall lead me, And Your right hand shall hold me.*
>
> Psalm 139:7-10

What makes his agony even more evident is the fact that he compares this misery to that of having every bone broken in his body. Picture if you will, trying to do the simplest of tasks, knowing that with every movement pain will shoot through your entire body.

That is precisely how one feels when he has sinned against God. David's every movement, every thought, every word was a constant reminder of how he had failed God. Consider that his woes began when he decided to take just one day off. It took only one day to undo a lifetime of good. Not just any day, but an evil day filled with enough leaven to . . . *leaven the whole lump* (Gal. 5:9). I think what is more frightening is the fact that this could happen to any one of us who, for whatever reasons, will not put on the armor of God daily. Whether we choose not to because of sin or neglect, either way the result will be the same, an experience that you would not wish upon your worst enemy.

As far as evil days go, we think about them as much as we think about how grass grows or about as much as we wonder how many stars there are in the sky. Like cancer, AIDS, horrible automobile accidents, and the like, we always believe that they will happen to someone else, but not us. I too fell into that trap, because after being somewhat victorious in God in whatever came my way for almost thirty years, I thought that He would neither . . . *leave me nor forsake me* (Heb. 13:5). What I was to find out later was that in all my experiences in God, I had never even come close to experiencing an evil day.

Life Before My Evil Day Began

Every marriage has its problems, and mine was no different. Of course, the best part of fighting was always making up and at least that option was always available. It is not my intention here to belittle, degrade, humiliate, pass judgment on, or expose Gloria's (my ex-wife's) private life for personal gain. It is with her permission that I write the following. Life had always been difficult for her. Being raised in a large family meant that her clothes were usually hand-me-downs. Working in the fields was not an option, but a necessity, accepting the fact that the family would have to move every summer and then again in the winter to follow the work. Her mother divorced her father when they were young, and growing up without him was a huge loss. Like most of her sisters, my ex-wife is fair to look upon, actually beautiful, but even this caused problems, because almost all of them, including her, were sexually abused. Giving her life to Christ and being filled with His Spirit made life bearable, so we fell in love and we married in August of 1975.

We were counseled by our pastor that there would be a period of adjustment. How long that would take would be determined by our personalities, our character, and our willingness to change. I had to be very patient with her sexual issues. There were times when she would wake up in the middle of the night screaming. The sexual abuse was being relived in her nightmares, and I would have to hold her close many times until she cried herself to sleep. If I had a desire to make love, it usually came at a time when her mind was still wrestling with her past. That meant that I would have to go without and somehow deal with it. Believe me, it happened quite often. In those early years God gave me a lot of patience and understanding, coupled with a lot of compassion for her, so I was able to manage things quite well.

The next few years brought a lot of growth in our marriage, because we were completely dedicated to the things of the Lord and each other. Our children were born at this time (Timothy,

Stephanie, and Christi), and although we had to cope with the disaster of a failed pastorate, I felt strongly that we had still gotten over the "hump." Even now I remember one time while on the road, in my hotel room, I uttered to myself that life had sure gotten good. We were not rich but for the first time in twenty years of marriage, we owned our own home and were not struggling financially as we had in the past. With a ministry that was flourishing, a marriage that got better with each and every day, great kids, and a God who loved me, what else could a man want? I continued to say that if I had to live like this for the rest of my life, that would be okay with me. It was several months after that statement was made that my evil day began.

A Surprise Like No Other

The new millennium, the year 2000, was supposed to usher in a continued prosperity for my family and me. There were plans made to get my wife back into ministry, this time involving our children with her. With Timothy playing the keyboard, my wife and Christi would resume singing on the praise team. Stephanie was to team up with her mom to teach Sunday school and boy could her Momma teach!

These plans never materialized, because in February of that year our marriage began to unravel. It had been several months before that Gloria's desire for sexual intimacy had completely gone through the roof. At the outset it was a welcomed change, but as her cravings to make love could not be satisfied, it really began to worry me. As a diabetic, things for me had slowed down quite considerably, and I had a hard time keeping up with her. It got to the point that we thought that maybe she was going through her change of life, so we had a doctor examine her. The tests were negative, which really began to scare me because I wasn't sure how I was going to be able to handle the new Gloria. As I prayed, there was no immediate clear cut answer, so I kept on seeking God.

Weeks passed by and out of nowhere her cravings came to an abrupt stop. The woman who could not keep her hands off of me was now very standoffish when it came to the bedroom. It was as if she had returned to her old ways, but in my spirit there was some thing different about her. If there's one thing that I have learned about a person who is prophetically gifted, it is that when dealing with family, the revelation isn't as obvious. There were situations in the family that, had I known before the tragedy struck, a whole lot of heartache could have been avoided. What I had learned was this: if I had been allowed to intervene on my family's behalf when everything was going south, then God would have been out of a job. If a lesson needs to be learned by us, then it is best learned when we deal with God directly. The only way we can recognize the voice of God and learn His ways is day-by-day, walking side-by-side, and getting back up when we fall.

The Lord was allowing Gloria this opportunity by making Himself available for whatever she needed of Him, but the sensual thoughts that for quite some time had taken over her mind got the better of her. It was under this huge pressure that she made a decision to break her marriage vows and commit adultery.

The next six months brought a literal hell to our entire family, because the sin went hidden for that period of time. Physically, Gloria was falling apart. Great clots of blood, caused by anxiety, would plunge to the shower floor as she bathed herself. Of course, the doctors could not find anything wrong physically. That same anxiety brought on even more irritation when dealing with us. It was at this time, I believe, that one of my children tried to commit suicide. I tried to take the brunt of all that was wrong, hoping to redirect Gloria's tirades away from the children toward me. I will never forget the counsel that she had received from a so called Christian counselor. The advice was to make sure that I was never to be told. Even a new convert will tell you that hiding sin from God and from authority is not God's way.

He who covers his sins will not prosper, But whoever confesses and forsakes them will have mercy.

                                                    Proverbs 28:13

Solomon's advice was not taken, and it was only a matter of time that the sin would be uncovered and officially our evil day would begin.

Our Evil Day Begins

It began on August 9, 2000, twenty-five years to the day we accepted vows to live together for the rest of our lives. Never in my wildest imagination did I believe that Gloria and I would ever separate. It was that day that Gloria could not continue to keep it a secret and told me what had happened and continued to happen for the next six months. To both of our surprise, my first reaction was not anger, but rather compassion. Because I knew my wife, how she was brought up, and how she reacted to failure, I knew that the next several months were going to be most difficult. I hugged her and held her close for a while, hoping with this show of support she would do the right thing. Leaving her lover and patching up our marriage relationship would be easier said than done. I knew that we were no longer at a level in God where we could just hide ourselves and ride off into the sunset. Nationally, in our organization, I had grown to a place that my ministry was well-known. Facing friends and family would mean suffering great humiliation, and I really wasn't sure if she could handle that. Sure enough, rather than face the music, she thought it best to separate, with the intentions of divorcing in the near future.

My evil day began with such a bang. I wish I could put into words the horrible feeling that I felt when Gloria said what she had to say. In a daze for weeks, my heart ached as if I myself had committed this sin. Even the simplest of tasks became a chore. Have you ever taken half an hour to button a shirt? I have. Starting at the top, you fumble and stumble till your mind goes off in a tangent. Staring in the mirror, you go back to the words that have caused so much heart ache. You wonder if they're really true, and the tears begin to well up in your eyes when you realize that they are. How long had you been standing there? Only God knows. You come back to reality to notice that you had only buttoned one button. The process continues on until *voila!* At least half an hour or more has been lost.

Having to be tested in every area of my life was quite taxing. The spiritual drought, social rejection, physical pounding, emotional distress, and financial loss all became a part of my evil day. The most challenging of the four had to deal with God hiding Himself (in my eyes) from me. I am a classic overachiever, and because I have not been blessed with the greatest of gifts, I have to work harder than most to be successful. That really didn't bother me when it came to the things of God (ie, prayer, fasting, etc.), because spending time with Him was always my delight. Obviously, more times than not, His manifest presence would be so awesome that it was easy to lose track of time as I sought more of Him. This was not true in my evil day. I felt as if my prayers would hit the ceiling then come crashing to the floor, as if to say, "You have been rejected by God, come back another day." After months of this sort of treatment, my self-esteem began a downward spiral that continued for the next four years.

Serving God would be so much easier if we didn't have to deal with people. If only we as His children could be as forgiving, patient, and kind, as He is. When the knowledge of my marital problems began to grow amongst our people, so did the lies, innuendo, half truths, and gossip. What made it even more difficult was the fact that in our organization, divorced ministers are not allowed to hold a ministerial license. There were some district officials who took it upon themselves to suspend my visitations to their area, just in case my marriage took that route. Others had been told that I already had been divorced and that the suspension was just a formality. I'm not talking about people that I didn't know. I'm talking about friends, pastors, and officials that I knew well; people that allowed me to minister in their churches in the past and were thankful that God had brought such a wonderful ministry to them. Now I understand David's words when he said,

> *Even my own familiar friend in whom I trusted, Who ate my bread, Has lifted up his heel against me.*
>
> Psalm 41:9

The more I tried to help people understand what was really going on in my marriage, the less people wanted to hear. In their eyes I was already guilty and at fault, so what was the use in hearing lies, anyway? Never in all the time that I had served God had I been rejected in this fashion. I had always made it a point to serve men the way I served God, and because of this my reputation was impeccable.

But I'm talking about an evil day, one where everything that you have done in the past is thrown out the window, and you are judged with incomplete information. The gossip had gotten so bad that living in Southern California was no longer possible. We sold our home just before we were going to lose it, the girls decided to stay with their mom, and Tim and I escaped to Central California.

The spiritual drought and the social rejection pretty much lasted the entire four years of the evil day. The other times of testing came in different increments. For an entire year, I suffered with a pain in the lower abdominal area. What made the enduring of this pain so grueling was the fact that my older sister, at the age of forty-eight, had just died with a similar pain. What was even more annoying was the fact that with all the tests that the doctors had taken, they too could not find anything physically wrong with me. The devil had a field day with this, and he began to terrorize me with death threats. "You'll die exactly like your sister died," he said, "and there's nothing God can do about it." With no support from the church and God being silent at this point, it made it very difficult to sort things out and know which way to go. But just like that, as mysteriously as the pain had showed up, after a year it was gone.

Having to move from an area that we had lived all our lives and given twenty-six years in ministry, I had broken the lines of communications completely. Pastors that were eager to invite me for meetings could not locate me, and my income suffered immensely. Needless to say, I knew that if my marriage did end in divorce, my license was not going to be renewed, and I would have to look for a secular job.

So as not to bear that embarrassment, I felt that I would bow out gracefully and find a job outside of the church. I didn't think twice about this, because I had earned a bachelor's degree in accounting and had held an emergency credential in the past to teach junior high math.

For the next two years, my efforts to find a job in accounting, teaching, or counseling were completely futile. I had never experienced anything like it, because in the past, whenever I had applied for a job, I always got it the first time. No matter how much I studied or prepared for interviews and/or tests, when the day did come to perform, my mind would go blank. The humiliation that I suffered trying to gain employment only forced me to continue to preach. I felt like I was between a rock and a hard place. The world didn't want me, but even sadder was the fact that neither did the church.

Like a beggar, I began to call pastors pleading to allow me to speak at their churches. Most of my efforts fell on deaf ears. Every once in a while, a pastor from a small congregation would give me a chance to speak. They had nothing to lose, so why not? Traveling hundreds of miles, because the surrounding districts had already banned me, my 1994 van, with almost three hundred thousand miles on it, remarkably got me to my destinations and back. There were times when pastors would take me out to eat. I would order an enormous amount of food. I know what they were saying in their minds, but I didn't care, because I was the taking leftovers home to give to my son.

I felt that if I was going to eat good at least once a week, well then so could he. When you don't have much to eat, you learn to appreciate anything and everything that is given to you. To this day, anytime I drive by an Arco gasoline station, I get emotional. At the height of our evil day, we could only afford one meal a day. That meant going down to the nearest Arco station and buying the best ninety-nine-cent hot dog you'll ever eat. I know they couldn't completely satisfy my son's hunger, but I always prayed that it would be enough to hold him for another day. For some funny reason, we never got tired of those hot dogs and to this day still haven't. Sometime later, my oldest daughter Stephanie came to live with us. She came to me one day and said, "Dad there's nothing to eat." Knowing that I didn't have any money to go to the market and buy food, instinctively I said, "God will provide." It just so happened that we had Bible study that night, and I had a class to teach. When we came home, what we beheld at our doorstep was mind-boggling. Someone had left a fifty-pound bag of beans (remember, we are part Mexican) with a gift certificate of one hundred dollars to one of the local markets. I hadn't mentioned our need to anybody, but God had. Somebody was sensitive to His Spirit and obeyed the voice of God, which became a huge blessing to us.

The Evil Day Continues

I'll never forget the year 2003. I know throughout our experiences in God there have been times that we thought what had come against us this time was going to be the one thing that would destroy us. It was at the beginning of this year that I finally began to fall apart emotionally. The evil day brought spirits of fear into my life in a manner that was new to me. By nature I am very fearful, and to think that Satan was allowed to use my weakness to bring even more fear was something that depressed me without measure. It was at this point that the fear was so overwhelming that I couldn't even get out of bed to pray. I was literally paralyzed so much that I earnestly implored God to forgive me for my unbelief, as my tears fell nonstop. Even my tears could not open the windows of heaven to pour out the blessing that I desperately needed. All day long the spirits would mock me, bringing about an enormous desire to sleep. I was hoping that I could avoid the unrest by closing my eyes, but the mayhem continued in the form of nightmares. I was averaging about three hours of sleep a night because the nightmares were even more intense than what I suffered through during the day. This lack of sleep created an incessant tiredness that had me feeling like a zombie 24/7. To this day I am astounded by the anointing that would flow powerfully through me when I had to preach on weekends. On the other hand, getting through the week was a different story. There were times that I would go to the living room and for no reason begin to cry. I felt so all alone and uncared for that, for the first time in my entire life, I wanted to die. I knew these thoughts were not my own, however, I felt helpless to do anything about it.

One day, as I was watching TV trying to get my mind off of this evil day, I saw a commercial about depression that brought some hope. I realized that all of the symptoms that were being named on this commercial were the exact same things that I was experiencing. Fortunately, a young man in our local church worked at a psychiatric hospital. I sought him out one day and began to tell him everything. He was willing to go to his boss, pretty positive that they would be able to do something for me. Unfortunately, he came back with an answer that I was not prepared for. After careful examination of all of the facts, his boss came to this conclusion. "Tell your friend," she said, "that we cannot help him, because he is a man of faith and his faith will save him." The problem was that I was tired of living the life of faith, and I just wanted some medication to help me sleep and calm me down. I was so miserable because of what I had heard that I made my way back to the apartment in utter despair, not knowing what to do next.

God Changes the Rules

The still small voice that I had longed to hear for so long began to whisper in my ear once again. He said, "Why don't you pray?" I thought to myself, *what for?* God had not been answering for the last three years, what would make me think that He would do so now? Trusting that the voice that I had heard was really God, I was willing to take one more step of faith and began to pray. He said, "Son, I still cannot end your suffering, because, in all honesty, you don't understand what an evil day is all about."

I responded with a hearty, "Oh yes, I do. An evil day is a time that includes confusion, heartache, and pain so severe that you would not wish it upon your worst enemy."

"You are about half right, but you still don't get it. It is because the suffering is not like any you have experienced, with Satan given the permission to do anything to you short of death, that I change the rules that will allow you to continue to be pleasing in My sight." He continued to say, "I understand that your strength and abilities during this time have been taken away, including your desire to do anything about it. That is why I only ask of you this one thing. Forget about ministry and muster up all of the strength that you have left so that you can stand in My presence with your sacrifice of praise."

For years we have welcomed the fact that our self-esteem comes from what we do for God. The more we delved into His work wholeheartedly, the more we believed He was pleased with us. That is why when ministry is taken away or for some reason is put on hold, we race with the greatest of determination to find our self-worth. That is why an evil day has such a profound effect on our psyche. No work on our part must mean that there is no love on God's part. I was so used to traveling all over the country with signs and wonders following, and the Lord filling powerfully with the Holy Ghost. How was I to accept the fact that I was still pleasing to God when I was no longer being used as frequently and as dynamically as before? It didn't take much to sink in, because as far as strength and willingness was concerned, I had little of both. So I made a decision to do as He was asking. Whatever my best was for that day, even if it didn't compare to what I had given to Him in the past, I would offer my sacrifice of praise, knowing that He would be pleased with it. With some getting used to, this new way of praising God started to pay dividends. My focus was no longer on my problems and when they were going to end, but more so on what I could do that would put a smile on the Master's face. The evil day did not end with this change in mindset, but it sure made things more bearable, easing my mind knowing that He still loved me, even when I couldn't do a thing for Him. I would like to leave one final note regarding the armor of God. Just because we decide to use it everyday does not mean that Satan will not attack. It is his job . . . *to steal, kill, and destroy* (John 10:10). So when his onslaught continues in the most difficult part of your evil day, don't worry when you're knocked down. Make sure that your armor is intact and with whatever strength you have left, no matter how long it takes, pick yourself up and stand in the presence of God. When you have done all that you can possibly do and your circumstances have not changed, know that God has not discarded you like a tattered old garment. He has just changed the rules, and there's only one thing that God requires of you in an evil day and that is to simply . . . STAND!

Chapter 5
While You Wait

Therefore the LORD will wait, that He may be gracious to you; And therefore He will be exalted, that He may have mercy on you. For the LORD is a God of justice; Blessed are all those who wait for Him.

Isaiah 30:18

You do not have to experience an evil day to dislike waiting. Because we usually misunderstand the purpose, most of us do not like to wait. In fact, this dislike often leads us to question the necessity of waiting. We might put up with waiting, but in reality we definitely don't like it. Knowing that God can do anything in our lives, it seems somewhat ludicrous that in times of trouble we have to wait on Him. We often ask, did He not form the world with the sound of His voice? Did He not speak into existence the beauty of nature and all that we have learned to enjoy? Wasn't it at His Word that we, His creation, were formed? Then, why in the world do we have to wait?

The answer may be found in two parts. First of all, in order for our faith to grow, it must be tested, and waiting will always test our faith. Remember that Hebrews 11:6 says ". . . *without faith it is impossible to please Him* . . ." This scripture tells us that faith is required if we are going to please our Father. God will at times put us in pressure situations, because the end result will be a growth in faith. The second reason why we have to wait is so that God's grace might be demonstrated through the waiting period.

Although we might understand the purpose behind waiting, waiting is still not fun. In fact, it is usually while we are in the waiting period that our faith, trust, and reliance in Him go out the window. Haven't you ever noticed that idolatry easily sets in while you wait? It is often during the time of waiting that we begin compromising our values, and question the relationship God wants us to have with Him. When our life in God has been put on hold, we readily make changes in our outward appearance, hoping that our new look will make things better. It is when we are waiting on God that our tastes for music become that much more worldly, what we watch becomes a bit more racy, and our interest in sports rises to a point where it flat out mesmerizes us.

In this sense, we are really no different than the Israelites. They, too, grew impatient waiting for the return of their leader Moses (Ex. 32). In the process of waiting, the Israelites threw away all that Moses had taught them and decided they would prefer to worship a god that they could see. With a unity that was rarely seen, they convinced Aaron to build them a god of gold, a golden calf. Living by faith was too much for them, so they took an easier route to serve God. Through their actions, the Israelites discarded all of God's instructions. Because the Israelites were tired of waiting, they allowed their own rationale to dictate their lifestyle choices. They lacked faith, and consequently were unpleasing in the sight of the Lord.

The biblical story of Moses reminded me of a time I attended a college football game with my son. As a sports fan, I am very careful in choosing how many games a year my son and I will go to. It's very easy to get caught up in the hoopla that surrounds the game itself, and I don't want to be guilty of giving my worship to anyone or anything besides my Jesus. I learned a great lesson a couple of years ago as my son and I went to see the USC versus Cal football game in Berkeley. It was the only game that USC was to lose in triple overtime during that season, and it just so happened that we were there.

Late in the third overtime as Cal began to drive for the winning score, the roar of the crowd became deafening. It was at this time that the Lord wanted my lesson to begin. I really wasn't interested, because it looked like USC was going down in defeat and I really wasn't in the mood. He asked me, "What do you hear?"

"What do you mean, what do I hear? I hear a bunch of crazy Cal fans about ready to explode, because they are going to upset the number three team in the nation, us!"

"No, no, no, what do you really hear?" He asked me again.

I stepped out of the moment to get into the Spirit and then it hit me like a ton of bricks. I responded somewhat embarrassed and sheepishly said, "I hear worship." It was a similar kind of worship that was heard throughout the camp of Israel when Moses descended from the mountain. The Lord had every right to wipe Israel off the face of the earth, but He didn't. The Israelites had discarded the truth. They put their faith in man rather than God. They worshipped something other than the Creator. For all the punishment that they deserved that day, God in turn was gracious to them.

God's Grace

What in actuality is grace? Nelson says that grace is favor shown without regard to worth or merit, and it's not deserved.

I have read stories of parents who shower their children with presents if they score the winning goal, if they bring home straight As, or if they stay out of trouble in school. These parents reward their children for their accomplishments, but if these same children don't do so well in the game, get a B on a test, or get in trouble in school, the wrath of the parents falls down. The praise of these parents is dependent on the accomplishments of the children. God's grace is different. He loves His children unconditionally. His grace is not dependent on the accomplishments of His people.

At times though, His children take advantage of this grace. The question I often ask myself is "Why would God exhibit such love, when it not only goes unnoticed, but also goes unappreciated?" How could Jesus die on the cross, knowing that His people, like the Israelites, would at times turn their back on Him?

Difference Between Grace and Mercy

Isaiah writes to us that once the Lord has been gracious to us and we acknowledge His grace, without being forced, He will be exalted (worshiped) in our life. This exaltation then allows the mercy of God to establish itself in a way not known to us. The snag that is found in most of our lives is the fact that we don't know the difference between mercy and grace. We constantly mix the two up, believing they are one and in the same. The difference between mercy and grace is simply this: grace comes when God makes the first move. It cannot be asked for, begged for, or prayed for. God showers His grace upon us when He feels like it, with no reason to do so. He does it because He's God and He can. In contrast, according to Isaiah, mercy comes when we exalt God. The results of grace and mercy are basically the same, the blessing of God falling upon one with a great need.

For anyone reading this book at this moment with a true understanding of what I have just written, you should be doing cartwheels right about now. Knowing that the answers to our problems can be determined by our worship, and not just waiting for God's grace to kick in, should bring an excitement to us like never before. If the answers to our problems have been put in our hands, then why is there so much despair and defeat in the lives of most Christians? The solution to this dilemma is found in a mindset that has been passed on now for generations. Going back to the scripture in Isaiah 30, we must return to the King James Version to fully understand where we have been missing it. The New King James Version states that God is the God of justice, a much more positive approach than the God of judgment application found in the original King James Version.

From as far back as the '50s, in own my experience, the focus of the church was to condemn and judge. Grace, forgiveness, and restoration were not words used in everyday life, as the church tried as hard as it could to keep sin at arm's length. What I found about this God of judgment was that literally in the Hebrew it was saying that God was a determined God (*misphat*). He is a God that does not readily quit on His children and has a mind made up for us to succeed. This is why He wrote these words through the prophet Jeremiah:

> For I know the thoughts that I think toward you, says the LORD, thoughts of peace and not of evil, to give you a future and a hope.
>
> Jeremiah 29:11

Reality Versus Perception

How sad that most of us at one time or another believed that God was in heaven having it in for us, just waiting for us to fail. If there was ever a lie that has sprung from the pits of hell, it is that. Not only is God continually thinking good, positive things about us, His thoughts reach into the future so that our success will also continue. This frame of mind not only stunted the growth of the early church, but it continues to hinder the move of God even today. Tradition dies hard and is not easily shattered. If there were ever a man that had room to dismiss the mercy of God and His forgiveness, it was Legion (Mark 5:1-20). Mark writes to us that the odds for Legion to succeed were stacked against him. Having lost his mind, controlled by thousands and thousands of demons, he lived in the tombs amongst the dead, wreaking havoc on all who passed by. He was too strong to be chained down and too wild to be controlled. His bloodcurdling screams at night struck much fear in those that would have liked to restrain him.

And then Jesus came to town. Somehow or another from afar Legion recognized that this man was the Son of God and proceeded to do something quite out of character for him. He made a mad dash toward the Master to worship Him. It was Legion's worship that caught the attention of the Lord. In turn, Jesus cast out all of the demons that had been tormenting Legion. Isn't that so awesome!!! Anyone and everyone who exalts the name of Jesus Christ will have the same results. The background of the person does not matter Legion was a man tormented by demons. God is a God who responds to our worship.

What is remarkable and quite sad is that we often have the faith to believe that God can do miraculous wonders in the lives of others, but, when it comes to us, our unbelief and at times our own condemnation wipes out any hope that God can do the same for us.

My Sister's Sad Story

My older sister Sally appeared to have it all. She was a pretty young lady, and, although somewhat overweight, it never seemed to stop the boys from calling. Sally had a great personality, one that drew people time and time again. She was so much like my father, who was in his own right a great salesman. They both had the gift of gab. Whereas my father could sell an air conditioner to an Eskimo in the coldest of winter, my sister could liven up even the most morbid gatherings around. Her sense of humor and wit usually had people in stitches. Her impersonations of others, especially of those in the church, always brought the house down. There was a spirit of hospitality that continuously drew people to her home, and once there they marveled at the way that she could decorate. She could have been an interior decorator if she wanted, but then again there were lot of things she could have been. That she was a great cook goes without saying. It did not matter to her that for years I had affectionately called her "ARNOLD" (the name for a pig on the television show *Green Acres* in the '60s). She had a magnet placed on her refrigerator door that was a reminder to all just how much she loved to cook. It simply said, "NEVER TRUST A SKINNY COOK!" It was a delight for her to have company with an opportunity to prepare another feast. It did not matter if you showed up late at night or in the wee hours of the morning, cooking meant SHOWTIME, just another chance to perform.

The children loved Auntie Sally the most, because she was the only one that could paint murals on their bedroom walls. Whether it was Strawberry Shortcake, Winnie the Pooh, or even the Oakland Raiders, nothing was too difficult for her to paint. Her way with children made it a natural for her to be an excellent Sunday school teacher. At the time that I was pastoring a new work, she was by far the best teacher that we had. Her teaching abilities did not stop in the classroom though. She was also blessed to be able to both sing and play the piano. When she wasn't getting the children ready for a Christmas musical or the like, she was writing her own songs, singing them in the Sunday night service. For all that she was able to accomplish, it seemed to be negated by the fact that she had a terrible time being faithful.

Leadership Misses the Boat

Those in leadership at the time were so baffled at her inconsistencies. There would be stretches of time that she would get lost in the shuffle, times where depression would dominate her every thought. This would cause a backsliding that later she would repent of, having to add it to the list of failures that would continue to trouble her spiritual life. Because they did not understand her, leadership decided to put her in the category of the rebellious, and consequently pretty much just left her alone. What they didn't understand was this: the root of all of her problems did not come from a rebellious spirit, it came from a tragedy that happened years ago that no one knew about. It was a secret that would be hidden from the family until years into her adult life. As a little girl, one of our uncles had sexually abused her. It was an ongoing thing that caused promiscuity problems in junior high that she just could not shake as she grew older. Giving her life to Christ had somewhat lessened the problem, but because it was still hidden, the nightmares continued. The embarrassment caused by her instability led her and her family to leave our organization to one with different beliefs.

She continued to make changes in her lifestyle, in her worship, and in the way that she served God, changes that I knew somewhere down the line were going to come back to haunt her. I feel I need to clarify some things before I go on. The way I serve God is not the only way that a person can make heaven their home. Because what I have received has come to me from revelation, I cannot fault anyone who has not come to the same knowledge of Christ as I have. It would be unjust to judge a person on something that he did not understand or comprehend. That being said, I also believe that once truth is revealed to a particular person, revelation cannot be undone. We will be made responsible for what has been revealed to us, and no matter who else is succeeding in ways that are different, we will be judged by how much light we have received. The book of James says it this way:

> . . . *Let not many of you become teachers, knowing that we shall receive a stricter judgment.*
>
> James 3:1

Why Such a Strong Admonition?

The warning was made clear and precise because James understood that God's people would not be judged all the same. He could also have included ministers, evangelists, pastors, bishops, apostles, etc, but the category of teacher includes all of these, and it would have only made his statement redundant. I don't think that it is a stretch to include believers also, because we are, at one time or another, teaching children, family, or even new converts. God would like to totally reveal Himself to all His children, not to just a precious few.

The relationship with my sister Sally was never the same. Although we would still visit every once in awhile, you could feel the tension and the uneasiness as we walked into her house. Her laugh was not the same, neither were her jokes. Every thought, word, or action was heavily guarded. Her new way of life in God did not bring the stability that she was looking for, and I believe this is what hurt her the most. Leaving everything that she had ever known took a great step of faith. To have it turn out the way it did certainly was unsettling. Coming back and admitting that it was a mistake would take an even greater step of humility, one that most people don't make.

I would now like to fast forward to three days before her death. For some time she had been going to the doctor for irregularities that she was experiencing in her body. The doctors could not find anything wrong with her, so with a clean bill of health they sent her home. It was at this time that the Lord troubled my mom's spirit so much so that she asked Sally to allow her to stay with her until she got better. Never in the thirty years or so that my sister was married did my mom ever spend the night. In prior chapters I talked a little bit about my dad and how charismatic he was in personality. My mom was the complete opposite. She spoke usually only when she was spoken to. I think of all of her sisters, six in all, she was the quietest. I am very much like my mom in personality, but that's not all we have in common. My mom was a great prayer warrior, and it is when she got into the presence of God that her quiet ways were lost. It wasn't uncommon for her to spend hours at a time, weeping before the Lord, interceding for those in need. If there was ever any one thing that was passed on to me from my mother that I appreciate more than anything else, it was her prayer habits.

On the morning that my sister died, she woke up with pain and shortness of breath. She immediately called for my mother, and she in turn asked my brother-in-law to give me a call. With great emotion, he asked me to come and pray for my sister. "There is something terribly wrong and you need to come as soon as possible," he cried out. I told him that at the moment I did not have any transportation but as soon as I could, I would be there. Immediately after I hung up, a great urgency to pray fell upon me, and I hurried to my room to intercede on her behalf. During this time of intercession, the Lord gave me a vision that began to calm my distressed soul. I saw her with hands raised, tears streaming down her cheeks, and with all of her heart speaking in other tongues as the Spirit gave the utterance. I had interpreted that to mean that when the time came I would to go to her house to pray, God would heal her, and she would make a comeback to God in the way that she had known before.

But that was not to be. In the meantime, without panicking at all, my mom got my sister by the hand and said, "Sally, it's time to pray." My sister knew what was coming next, and it made her feel quite uneasy. Every prayer that my mom had ever made meant that she would touch God in the Spirit, speaking in other tongues. As my sister tried to make mom understand that she no longer prayed in that fashion, my mom would not take no for an answer. She grabbed my sister by the hand, lifted it to the sky and let loose. Within minutes she was in the presence of God and a glory cloud filled the room. It was moments later my sister followed her and together they took advantage of the splendor and grandeur of God Himself.

She was finally in the place where no one could hurt her. A place that she was accepted just the way she was. Finding herself once again in the arms of God, she died giving Him the glory. A half an hour had passed since the phone call from my brother-in-law. The next voice I heard on the phone was my mom, telling me that moments ago my sister had died.

I was so confused, because I honestly thought that not only would she be healed but better yet, make a comeback that would bring the family back together. When I finally was able to get to my sister's house several hours later, most of the family was there being very distraught with me. They were of the opinion that if I had arrived in time, God would have used me to heal her and she would not have died. I am aware of the fact that many times God had used me to pray for people that the doctors had already given up on. These diseases had no remedies; they were diseases that gave no hope. Yet every time God had chosen me to lay my hands on them for healing, there was always one thing that I was constantly reminded of. Whether it was the blind, deaf, those stricken with AIDS, or cancer victims, I knew that I was only an earthen vessel, one that allowed the Spirit of God to flow freely. Yes God could perform the miraculous through me, but I WAS NOT GOD.

Looking for a Confirmation

My mom took me into the room where she was. As I looked at her it appeared as if she was sleeping. Various thoughts began to race through my mind. Not only did I have to reconcile the misinterpretation of the vision that I had had, I also was aware that I would have to deal with a possible change in mindset. For years we had been taught that once a member of the church left, heaven for them was not an option. I was ready to defend that position, even though that meant that my sister would be affected. I desperately needed to hear from God to see if a new lesson was to be learned here in her death. I left the room for a few moments to gather my thoughts. As I tried to avoid the rest of the family that had now become somewhat agitated with me, I prayed silently under my breath. Up to this point in ministry, God had always been good about giving me confirmations of what He wanted me to do. As I frantically searched for one, the Lord spoke to me verifying that once I returned to the room, the confirmation that I was looking for would be right before my eyes.

Before I share with what the Lord had revealed, looking back on my sister's life, I realize now just how much suffering she was willing to endure. Her depressions took her to such dark and dreary places that at times I would find her alone in a completely darkened house, staring into space with tears running down her cheeks. The life of the party was such a different person when she was alone. Miserable, unhappy, down in the dumps, dejected, disheartened, sad, glum, despondent, adjectives that impeccably described how she felt. Choose any of those adjectives, plug them in at one time or another and they would fit perfectly. She was so good at hiding it in public, but in the privacy of her home away from public opinion, what she really thought about herself was killing her. Her God was a God of judgment and how could she escape His wrath with all the wrong that she had done? It didn't matter that God had already forgiven all of her past transgressions, and had forgotten them as well. The belief that God was also a God of mercy, forgiveness, and restoration never had the opportunity to find a lodging place in her heart. Consequently, her life was always lived in fear. For one brief moment, as she entered into the presence of God for one last time, she found the peace that she had always been looking for. It was at that moment that she died, with her rejoicing to continue in heaven.

I entered her bedroom with great fear, because I really wasn't sure what I was going to encounter. I was willing to defend what we had been taught, but I was also hoping that there was something God would show me that would confirm that someday I would see my sister again in heaven. I took one last glance at my beloved older sister, and everything that I had seen the first time was pretty much the same except for one glaring difference. The Lord had put a smile on her face. For all that she had suffered, for all that she had endured, God's way of expressing Himself with that smile was more than an exclamation point. Ecstatic with His confirmation, I said my last goodbyes, bidding farewell to my one and only "ARNOLD."

Pretty mushy stuff, huh? I know that experience and revelation do not override God's Word. There has to be something in the Scriptures that will confirm what I have just written. It is so much easier to hide behind traditional beliefs that were either never based on the Word of God or believed by its misinterpretation. For those of you that believe that my sister did not merit the grace of God to be forgiven before she died, for example's sake, I will agree with you. Living for God and then backsliding time and time again was not God's idea of how we, His children, should serve Him. But God in His infinite wisdom knew that there was another way to touch His throne, calling a quiet, little mother who knew how to worship. When my mom got my sister to exalt the name of Jesus, what in reality they were doing was invoking the scripture in Isaiah 30:18. Isaiah could not have written it in any plainer. "MERCY ALWAYS COMES TO THOSE WHO WORSHIP GOD." When she took her last breath that day and entered into eternity, it was mercy, not grace, that escorted her to heaven.

Concluding Thoughts

Let us return to Isaiah 30:18. The verse simply says that the Lord will wait, and He will be gracious to you. The Lord waited for my sister Sally, and, although she died, He was gracious to her. When Sally lifted her hands in worship with my mother, the Lord was exalted, and He had mercy upon her.

Worshiping God through an evil day may not be the easiest of things to pull off, but all the same, it's God's way.

Therefore the LORD will wait, that He may be gracious to you; And therefore He will be exalted, that He may have mercy on you. For the LORD is a God of justice; Blessed are all those who wait for Him.

Isaiah 30:18

Chapter 6
I Choose To Defer

The discretion of a man deferreth his anger; and it is his glory to pass over a transgression.

Proverbs 19:11

The latter portion of this scripture begins by talking about a person's glory. What is it exactly that we are looking for when we define a person's glory? By Webster's definition, *glory* is "something that distinguishes a person from others." It is a trait that stands out, glows bright enough to be noticed by all, and is a part of our lives that we take special pride in. For example, a man's glory is his wife (Prov. 12:4). A woman's glory is her hair (1 Cor. 11:15).

When talking in terms of the work of God, a person's glory is their ministry. It is Solomon's view of glory that we seem so out of touch with. According to the wisest man that ever lived, once a decision is made to put off (defer) one's anger, his glory will allow him to pass over a transgression. In other words, you can put off your rights until a later time, when your thinking is much more rational, allowing you to forgive much more easily than if you would have demanded judgment right on the spot. If you are having as much trouble accepting this concept as I did when God first dealt with me during the evil day, take a number. The Pharisees had a similar problem when Jesus spoke to a paralytic man one day.

> *When Jesus saw their faith, He said to the paralytic,*
> *"Son, your sins are forgiven you."*
>
> Mark 2:5

Most of us have been led to believe that the Pharisees were infuriated because Jesus was making Himself out to be God. The problem was this: on this occasion Jesus was talking as a man and not as God. What really should have caused them to be up in arms was that Jesus, as a man, was setting a precedent. If forgiveness could be a characteristic of man, and not only of God, then they too as men would have to do the same. This was so foreign to them, because the law only had room for judgment and condemnation, but not for forgiveness. The true power of forgiveness is demonstrated in the words of Jesus:

> *"Which is easier, to say to the paralytic, 'Your sins are*
> *forgiven you,' or to say, 'Arise, take up your bed and*
> *walk'? But that you may know that the Son of Man has*
> *power on earth to forgive sins" He said to the paralytic,*
> *"I say to you, arise, take up your bed, and go to your*
> *house."*
>
> Mark 2:9-11

Unleashing the Glory of God
The Lord knew that the Pharisees would have difficulty responding to either question, because they had never forgiven

anybody, much less seen a miraculous healing. The key to verse 10 is the phrase "Son of Man." It is the phrase that Jesus constantly used to identify His human side. The power of forgiveness was going to be unleashed through His humanity. This is the lesson that Jesus was trying to teach all that were listening that day as the paralytic was healed. *FORGIVENESS ALWAYS UNLEASHES THE GLORY OF GOD.*

Time and time again, I've heard song leaders tell us that the glory of God is present in the house, as they try to take us to the throne of God in worship. All the while there are members disgruntled with each other. Husbands and wives are ready to split up, not seeing eye to eye. Children are rebelling against their parents, and the pastor is being ridiculed beyond measure. We are no different than the crippled man that sat close to the edge of the pool of Bethesda, waiting for the angel to move the waters (John 5:1-15). Knowing that the first one to jump in would be healed, they were always jostling for position. It did not matter who was being hurt by the ruckus, the bottom line was to jump into the pool before anyone else. It was not their intention to become more Christ-like when they received their healing; all they wanted was their prayer to be answered so they could go on with their life.

Sound familiar? If we truly allowed our forgiveness for others to unleash the glory of God, then we wouldn't be so inclined to be satisfied with a moving of His Spirit on Sunday afternoons. There also wouldn't be any disagreements among our members, nor potential breakups in marriages. Children would honor their parents in the Lord, and the pastor would be given honor to which he is due. The greatest benefit of God unleashing His glory would be the souls that would be saved in record number. As they would make their way into the glory-filled house of God, they too would say the same words of those that saw Jesus in action that day, "*We never saw anything like this!*" (Mark 2:12). It was His glory prompting them to be saved.

Moses Chooses to Defer

Knowing that deferring one's anger was the first step toward forgiveness did not make it any easier for Moses when he had to deal with his brother and sister. Miriam and Aaron were constantly ridiculing his wife. It got so bad that it became a part of Miriam's ongoing complaint. One of the greatest lessons that I have been able to glean from the life of Miriam is this: God can still use us mightily, even when our character flaws stick out like a sore thumb. She was not only a prophetess, but also a crowd favorite with her charismatic personality. Wasn't it Miriam that led the greatest conga line when the children of Israel escaped Egypt? You better believe it! Playing the tambourine like it was going out of style, she was determined to lead them out of captivity with a flair.

The Lord was not about to wait for Miriam's life to line up perfectly in every way so that she could do the work of God. In the interim, as God chiseled away at these flaws, Moses had to put up with his big-mouthed sister. After one of her legendary attacks on Moses' wife, God had seen enough and pronounced judgment upon her. He chose to make her a leper, the most embarrassing judgment a Hebrew could experience while being alive. This was so because becoming a leper meant that God had judged a horrible sin in your life, a judgment that was irreversible. For all intents and purposes, Moses was in his rights to let the hammer of God fall, allowing the Lord to even up all the losses he had suffered from his disrespectful sister. Putting his rights aside, he chose to defer. An overwhelming burden fell upon him so that he could intercede on Miriam's behalf, pleading to God for mercy.

In today's society, no one is willing to give up their rights, including those in the church. Whether African-American, Hispanic, or Indian, we all have rights. The willingness to fight for rights includes women, gays, children, handicapped, the poor, and so on, and so on, and so on. In the eyes of all Americans that have rights, Moses is viewed as a fool. Who in their right mind would give up any rights of leadership, especially when they were handed to you on a silver platter? Is it any wonder that there are so many problems in the church today? Very few are willing to humble themselves and to defer their rights so that the kingdom of God can grow.

Deferring our rights under all circumstances appears to be going a bit to the extreme. Does God expect us always to turn the other cheek, even when the attacks become personal? You know the ones that I mean. There are those confrontations that undermine your character, your integrity, and your motives. They continue to reach into your inner core with the ability to turn you inside out. You feel entirely defenseless because every attempt to defend yourself is futile. Your good works are viewed as evil, and your mistakes are blown out of proportion. Even your motives are judged as corrupt, as they leave no stone unturned. In this state we want our side to be heard so that the truth will be known, but no one will take the time to listen.

A Prayer Most of Us Won't Pray

A young deacon by the name of Stephen found himself in a similar predicament (Acts 6:8-7:60). He was chosen from the best of the best to help the apostles. He had a good reputation and was full of the Holy Ghost and wisdom. His credentials were impeccable, even to the point that he humbled himself to serve tables without complaining. After completing his daily responsibilities with joy and gladness not found in the others, he would then go out and preach the gospel with much success. There are always people around that will grumble about anything, and there was a group called the Libertines that could not handle Stephen's success. They stirred up the people, set up false witnesses, accused him of blasphemy, and then presented him before the council. Stephen began his defense of blasphemy by quoting scriptures in the Old Testament. Although his entire response to their questions was rooted in Scripture, they still convicted him to death. A strange thing transpired as they dragged him out of the city gates to die by stoning. As the rocks began to fly, he called on the name of the Lord. If there was ever a young man who had the right to pray to God for his life it was Stephen. He was just beginning to flourish in his ministry. Signs, wonders, and great miracles were becoming commonplace as he obeyed the voice of God. Even greater things were in store for him, and his future looked so bright. His life could not end like this, not here, not now. But his prayers were not like the ones that perhaps you and I would have prayed, because he did not pray for himself. After seeing the glory of God, his prayer became one of forgiveness.

> But he, being full of the Holy Spirit, gazed into heaven and saw the **glory of God,** and Jesus standing at the right hand of God, and said, "Look! I see the heavens opened and the Son of Man standing at the right hand of God!" . . . Then he knelt down and cried out with a loud voice, "Lord, do not charge them with this sin."
>
> Acts 7:55-56, 60

Stephen made one decision and only one. He chose to defer his anger, and with it the glory of God was unleashed. It took just one glimpse of God's glory for it to be transferred to the heart of Stephen. That is why, when Stephen uttered his last words, they sounded very similar to the ones that Jesus spoke before He died on Calvary's Cross.

> Then Jesus said, "Father, forgive them, for they do not know what they do."
>
> Luke 23:34

Alone, scared, perhaps not knowing what to do, but when the glory of God took full effect, there was given to him enough strength, courage, and the right words to overlook a transgression that would cost him his life. This was made possible because he made the decision to defer.

After scrutinizing every single move that Stephen made and analyzing it from every angle possible, I still have a hard time believing that the run of the mill Christian could accomplish what Stephen did. It became even more difficult to accept when Jesus came to me during my evil day asking to give up my right to be angry with Gloria. It had been four years now that my wife had decided to live a new lifestyle, one that would not include me. For all that I had suffered, for all that had been lost, I knew that if I were the only one affected by her decision that somehow or another with time I would find the means to forgive. The problem was this, the pain of separation found its way into the hearts and lives of our children.

The Deepest Pain to Endure

It's one thing having to endure pain, heartache, misunderstandings, and loss. It's another thing when your children are dragged into the same mess. Having Timothy (my son) decide to stay with me was a Godsend, on my part anyway. If I would have had to go through the evil day without him by my side, I would never have made it. Sad to say, being so far away from his mom and sisters disturbed him deeply. He had a hard time communicating with his mother, because she was rarely at home. When he was able to get through, the conversations were usually short and somewhat curt. Because of his lack of understanding, he could not comprehend why his mom was pushing him away when he needed her the most. This caused a lot of guilt, anger, and frustration. These emotions became so strong that it affected his schoolwork big-time. His grades fell below the average that he needed to be able to qualify for scholarship money, and this consequently added to our financial problems. I tried to explain to him that his mom was confused and that in time everything would get back to normal. Oh, how I wanted to believe that so badly, but if I couldn't even convince myself, surely Timothy wasn't buying it. According to him, the *consentido* (the Spanish translation for "the favorite") had lost his place, and perhaps would never find it again.

My daughters were another story. Gloria had never lied to them, but then again half-truths can have the same effect. Out of nowhere, my girls became very hostile towards me. Just to be with me in the same room at times turned their stomach, and I just didn't understand why. I tried to ask what was going on, only to be greeted with blank stares and a halfhearted, "Nothing." You have to understand that for the longest time they were "daddy's girls." Growing up, when they needed somebody to show them how to ride their bikes, I was there. When it came to going to the park or racing over the "wheeeeeeee" bridge, guess who got the job? Why, of course, me, daddy-o. Whether teaching them how to dribble and shoot a basketball, or trying to explain the intricacies of serving a volleyball, I was always the one to do it. One of my greatest accomplishments raising my girls was when I got to do my James Bond impersonation. Sneaking the kids out for an ice cream or candy and getting home safely without being caught by "Big Momma" was a feat that would have made 007 proud.

Of course, when it comes to spiritual things, there was nothing that made me prouder than when I laid hands on my girls and God filled them with the baptism of Holy Ghost. When they decided at different times to be baptized in water, I not only did the honors, but I also got to preach the message too. I remembered in my preparation that I wanted the messages to be special, and they were. Stephanie's was entitled "When My Princess Becomes a Queen," and Christi's was entitled "Trading Angel Wings for a Master's Crown." I have promised myself that I will never preach them again, solely because it was my personal message to them. With all of that in mind, it was killing me that my daughters didn't want to have anything to do with me. It finally came to a head one Thanksgiving weekend, when all of us began to share what was on our heart. When it came to my time to share, fighting the tears was a losing battle. I tried the best that I could to explain what had happened between me and mom, and when I was finished, they, too, were in tears. Although we were able to patch things up, there was still one thing left that had not been resolved that, when I thought about it, made my blood boil. Their walk with God had been put on hold, with no immediate plans to get back on track. They were given liberties that were reserved for adults, and it was only a matter of time before they, too, would get into trouble. Without biblical training, their views on life became the ones that they saw on television or read in worldly magazines.

I don't hold anything against them for choosing an easier way of life. I probably would have done the same thing if I were to be put in the same situation. The one thing that I must admit though is that the pain that I must endure seeing my daughters not serving God is a pain greater than any that I have ever experienced. I realize now that our divorce has so affected them that they have had second thoughts about getting married themselves. These are some of Christi's thoughts on marriage, which she put in a paper that helped her win first prize in a district essay contest:

A Loss of Faith

When we take our vows and say I do, it's supposed to be forever right? To my great dismay, I've learned that forever just isn't what it used to be. As a young girl, I thought marriage was like a wonderful fairytale, and I was just waiting for my prince to come. I used to think that married people had a bond that could never be broken. Although when we say our vows on our wedding day you may mean it then, sadly, people change and grow apart. All my life while growing up I saw the marriages of my friends fall apart, and I thought how lucky I was because that could never happen to me. I was the person that my friends envied because my parents were still together for so long and still going strong. I had a great childhood with a loving family who gave me wonderful memories. Every Saturday we would spend the day at the park of our choice and eat at the restaurant of our choice. I can remember thinking how great I thought my parents' marriage was and how I was going to have one just as great. It seemed that my world of bliss began crumbling in the beginning of my eighth-grade year. I couldn't comprehend everything that was going on. How do you stop loving someone after 25 years? I felt so deceived! How could this happen when I thought my parents were so happy? Of course as the year went on, I didn't even want to be home. Not only were my parents having marital problems, my dad thought it would be best to move up north as if everything would magically change and become better. My life was crumbling before me, and there was nothing I could do but to cry.

Now I am 17, a senior, and live with my mom. Due to my parents failed marriage and failed marriages of those closest to me, I am very apprehensive about getting married. On your wedding day no one has the intention of getting divorced. When you're in love, It seems you've turned into a raving optimist, which realistically, can cloud your judgment on reality. Sadly, now I am a bit of a pessimist when it comes to marriage. I almost never want to get married because what's the point if you're just going to get divorced? Life taught me that love and marriage isn't a fairytale and not everything is going to end up happily ever after.

The thought of marriage for me just isn't what it used to be. Instead of happy thoughts of finding   Mr. Right, I'm constantly trying to detect if he's Mr. Wrong. I thought marriage was forever and unbreakable, but life taught me otherwise. Now when I think of marriage, I just think of divorce. It's sad to know that most people nowadays are divorced when there was a time when divorce was unheard of. Marriage now seems like it's not even worth it, but one day I hope I'm proven wrong and someone can show me that I can be loved and that marriage can last for ever.

Is it any wonder that God hates divorce?

For the LORD God of Israel says that He hates divorce.
Malachi 2:16

Why God Hates Divorce

Not so much for the couple that is involved, but even more so for the rest of the family that has to suffer needlessly. There are far-reaching effects placed upon the children that parents don't take into consideration, and because of this, divorce has become just as common in Christian homes as it is in non-Christian homes. That being said, can you understand now why I wasn't willing to defer my anger towards my wife? I hated her with every fiber in my body. Oh, how I hated her! My words don't even come close to trying to describe the emotions that I have felt towards her. I had never felt like this about anybody in my entire life, because by nature I am a very forgiving person.

The devastation of my children finally brought to the surface a hate that I never thought was possible. If anything, I wanted vengeance, not forgiveness. This desire began to consume my every thought, and why not? I was within my rights, so I thought. His reply was a forceful one when He said:

> *"Vengeance is Mine, I will repay," says the Lord.*
> Hebrews 10:30

The Lord wanted to handle it, and as difficult as that was to swallow, having to defer my rights seemed so out of the question. I remember pleading with Him to take back His request. The damage had been so deeply rooted that there wasn't anything that could be done to stop the pain. I had gotten to the point that I just wanted her to hurt as much as I was hurting, and I really didn't care how it happened. In my mind, she deserved the most excruciating, agonizing, dreadful pain a person could experience on the face of the earth, and because of this forgiveness was just not feasible.

The First Step to Forgiveness

It was with that kind of attitude that the Lord nudged me again asking me to defer. He then went on to explain that He was not asking me to forgive. He said that asking one of His children to forgive when their heart had been shredded to pieces was cruel and unusual punishment, something that He would never ask. "The first step to forgiveness is to first of all defer your rights and anger," said the Lord. "All that I am asking," He continued, "is for you to make a decision, one that will hand over to Me the responsibility to make everything right." I argued that I felt that it was impossible for me, at the drop of a hat, to just let go of my feelings and to become numb to my hurt. Furthermore, after exhausting all my strengths and efforts to get by during this evil day, I didn't have anything left to complete such an enormous request. He gently uttered, "That is My problem, not yours; I just need for you to make the decision." *And He said to me,*

> *"My grace is sufficient for you, for My strength is made perfect in weakness."*
>
> 2 Corinthians 12:9

I tried to go back at various times in my Christian life, to see if in fact God's grace had been sufficient in times of weakness. Knowing that grace is always God-initiated and cannot be requested by us puts a great strain on one, because we are not in control. My objections were finally put to rest when He brought this back to my memory. Let's see if you can identify.

As we have begun a particular journey traveling in this Christian walk, every once in awhile there will be a spiritual pothole that has the opportunity to take us out. In our dismay, no matter what we do, it appears that we are not going to be able to get out. Then, out of nowhere, there is an incredible force that picks us up, and with renewed strength, we are able to continue. The journey is a long one and quite grueling, so the process is repeated over and over again. As we finally reach our destination, victorious over every obstacle, there's still one question that boggles the mind. As we are allowed to turn around and see just how far we've come, we ask, "How in the world did we ever make it?" God simply replies, "With my grace." Try to explain it as much as you will, but you just can't explain grace. It is God-ordained, God-designed, and God-meant, with all of the explanations of "how" hidden in the portals of heaven.

With as much faith as I had when I responded to the call of God to become an evangelist (almost none), I made my decision to defer. It was only one decision; however, it will be a decision that I will never forget. After a period of time, and I really don't know how long, every physical pain, mental anguish, ill feelings, and the like toward Gloria were gone. I wish to God I could explain to you how I did it, but I can't. If there was ever a touch of God initiated by His grace, it was here, in my evil day. It was God's intention for me to get to this place, so that now that we talked about forgiveness, I would be more willing to do that.

A Glory Unheard Of

Being at peace with myself meant that forgiving Gloria was just a formality. The problem was this: I was feeling so good that I thought that maybe I had done something wrong. So I did what had become a custom of mine during the evil day, and that was to go to others for counsel. The advice was nearly always the same: they thought it quite noble that I was willing to forgive Gloria, but felt it out of the question to resume the marriage. Only because there was a check in my spirit did I choose to see what God had to say about the situation Himself. It was in this prayer that God had revealed a great change in me that would be a part of me from here on in. He said, "Son, the reason that they do not understand you is because this thing called forgiveness has become your **GLORY**. Your decision to defer allowed my Spirit to deal with you in ways that were not possible up to this point. And because you have allowed yourself to be vulnerable to outside influences, I have deposited in you something that few people have received. As time goes on, you will shine brighter and brighter, being the earthly example that I need to show my children what true forgiveness is." It is incredible how God has the ability to wipe away the hardness of heart with just one decision. I have witnessed firsthand the true glory of God, and no one can take that away from me.

The sun is now starting to set on my evil day, and although it's not completely gone, the most difficult part is behind me. Still up ahead are the problems to be dealt with in the aftermath of divorce. Earlier in the year 2005, after five years of separation, Gloria filed for divorce. How will it affect my children, my ministry, and most important my relationship with God? Only God knows.

Chapter 7
God Still Uses What Is Left

"For I will restore health to you And heal you of your wounds," says the LORD, "Because they called you an outcast . . ."

Jeremiah 30:17

And the priest shall pour some of the oil into the palm of his own left hand.

Leviticus 14:26

Looking at both scriptures above, in discussing the evil day, it is easy to understand why the first one is there. But what does the left hand have to do with moving on and being restored once again? Let's take some time in discussing the left hand and see if we can find out.

Historically, the left hand has had a bad rap. It gets so bad that in some cultures, its use has been banned. It was hilarious to see how hard my wife tried to get my son to stop using his left hand (he's a lefty, just like his dad). When he would pick up his food to eat, she would always switch that food to the right hand. He would just wait till she left and switch over to the left, which allowed him to eat faster. To this day he still eats very fast.

Lefties have always been considered outcasts, oddballs, weirdos, etc. Lefties forever have been told to adjust, conform, alter, modify, or change their ways. Because most people in the world today are right-handed, they don't realize that we live in a right-handed world.

Because of my handicap, with my right arm being withered, I had to learn how to play the trumpet left-handed. When I went to band class for the first time, the instructor told me that I had everything backwards, but when he realized that there was no strength in my right hand, he allowed me to play that way, so as not to discourage me (one year later I was first chair in the entire district).

When I started to study accounting and became aware that I would have to master the adding machine, doing it left-handed was quite a chore, because all adding machines are made for use with the right hand. I'll never forget the first day of college, when I went to the bookstore to buy my books. Low and behold they were actually selling notebooks for lefties. I thought I'd died and gone to heaven, because all lefties know how much of a struggle it is writing in a right-handed notebook. Be it ever so subtle, the demand for conformity is still there.

The Left Hand in Scripture

As the Lord began to talk to me about the left hand, I thought that scripturally I would be able to find something positive. Sadly to say, most of the scriptures that I did find were just as negative as the worldly point of view. The book of

Judges said that using the left hand showed weakness (Judg. 3:15). According to Jonah 4:11, the use of the left hand shows immaturity. The author in Ecclesiastes goes as far as to say that its use is improper (Eccles. 10:2). Matthew throws the final dagger in the use of the left hand by saying that it is flat out evil (Matt. 25:33). The only scripture that I found that had a halfway positive meaning was the one that I found in Song of Solomon 2:6, which said at best it was a woman's preference. When I found out the literal meaning of using the left hand, it only got me more depressed. Unger's Dictionary says it literally means in Hebrew ('itter yad-yemino) "shut as to the right hand." The only reason the left hand was being used was because there was something wrong with the right hand, or at best you were just being deviant.

Being frustrated as I was, I really didn't understand what God was trying to say. As I was about to give up, I found a couple of scriptures in Ezekiel that brought a ray of hope. Ezekiel 4:4, 6 states that the left hand helps to complete the right hand. Without the help of the left hand, the right hand becomes deficient. On its own, the right hand is the hand of power and authority; but without the help of the left hand, its power is diminished and its authority undermined. It is the use of the left hand that allows the right hand to become so dominant.

A Hidden Truth

When the priest in the Old Testament began to make sacrifices before the Lord, there was an assortment of procedures that had to be undertaken. Slowly and methodically, the priest had to complete each procedure in the exact way that the Scriptures had commanded. When he offered a trespass offering, according to Leviticus 14, the priest had to fill his left palm with oil (oil has always been a type of the anointing). This allowed him to use the right hand for ministry (ie, sprinkling). In order to complete the work, both hands were to be used. The spiritual significance of this was that the filling of the left hand with oil was a type of consecration. The Lord revealed this to me when He asked me to look up the definition of *consecrate*. I found two definitions amongst the many that would help me uncover a hidden truth. The Hebrew word *male* (maw-lay) means "to take a hand full." The word *yad* (yawd) means "left hand." If we take the two definitions separately and put them together this is what we get: TAKE A LEFT HAND FULL. What God was trying to get across to us was simply this: in order for our ministry to be effective, before we even get started, we MUST first be consecrated.

We reject consecration pretty much the same way we avoid using the left hand. It's awkward, unfamiliar, and all it does at best is slow us down. We say we don't pray because we don't know how. We see fasting as nothing more than a type of starvation. When it comes to study of the Word of God, in our minds, it's all Greek. Rejecting our consecration to Him is like rejecting God Himself.

> *Have you not even read this Scripture: "The stone which the builders rejected has become the chief cornerstone."*
> Mark 12:10

Consecration has become the cornerstone of our existence. Rejecting it would make us deficient and unbalanced. You can't serve God if you don't know Him, and you cannot know Him without consecrating yourself unto the Master.

The Story of David

David's group of mighty men was powerful, fearless, and unrelenting. They were a mirror image of their leader, both in battlefield savvy and in their worship habits. They were truly a well-oiled fighting machine. 1 Chronicles 12:1-7 tells us that a new group of warriors joined David at Ziklag. They were a group of Saul's men, men that had left Saul to come and help David. Reading the Scriptures, we were already told that

David's men were mighty warriors. The question that we need to ask is: What could David possibly need from the fighters that he already didn't have? In other words, what value did he see in Saul's men?

The unique characteristic that they brought to the table was the fact that Saul's men fought expertly with both hands. Bows and arrows, hurling stones, it didn't matter, their skills were unmatched by anyone. What made them so valuable was the fact that they would initially go into battle right-handed. With the enemy confident that they were in command of the battle, they would switch their weapons to the left hand without warning, confusing the enemy, giving them an unfair advantage. An enemy confused is an enemy defeated.

<u>Today's Church</u>

The church lives in an age where we are so power hungry. We seek the power gifts that are found in the right hand, believing that these gifts will be the difference in our battles against Satan in spiritual warfare. The obstacle that we encounter is this: Satan does not fear anything that we throw at him with our right hand. It is only when we get that right hand and dip it into our oil-filled left hand that the anointing has an opportunity to super size and supercharge our gifts. Now Satan is put at a disadvantage, because as the scripture states, ". . . *the yoke will be destroyed because of the anointing oil* (Isa. 10:27)." In other words, it is our gifts coupled with the anointing of God that confuses the devil totally. Now another promise of God comes into play when He says this through Isaiah:

> *No weapon formed against you shall prosper . . . This is the heritage of the servants of the LORD.*
>
> Isaiah 54:17

Still think consecration is overrated? Why don't you do some finger dipping into the anointing and find out for yourself just how powerful and victorious you can become by using your left hand. The more you consecrate, the more the oil will flow, and with the oil flowing in times of crisis, that will be the determining factor in your success.

God Still Uses What Is Left Over

As powerful a lesson that can be learned from the left hand of anointing, there's yet another lesson that is as equally important, the one that GOD STILL USES WHAT IS LEFT OVER. When an evil day is in full bloom, like a hurricane spinning out of control, it destroys everything in its path. What was once safe, secure, and untouchable is no longer there, once an evil day has gotten done with it.

The best that we had to offer, the things that we prided ourselves in most, are now nothing more than mere rubble that cannot be replaced. Because of these losses, our whole world is in disarray. Nothing is automatic anymore, and much more thought is used just to complete the little things. Frustration now becomes our dancing partner, because life has thrown us a curve. We find it so easy to second-guess ourselves, kicking around in our heads the disaster that has befallen us. Reprimands find their place in line because we know that our stupidity has produced that foul taste in our mouth, so difficult to purge. Despite all the destruction, GOD STILL USES WHAT IS LEFT OVER.

Learning the Hard Way

Samson was a man that had a hard time deciding exactly what he wanted in this world. There were times that he took his job as the judge of Israel very, very seriously. Then there were times that, looking at him, it made you wonder what God was thinking when He had chosen this man to lead His children. Playing with fire will eventually burn you, and no one is exempt. When Samson began to fool around with the things of God, his sin caused his world to be shaken to its core. So careless was he that God could not withhold judgment from his life. He was so powerful in ministry, yet a weakling in his consecration. The cutting of his hair was only a confirmation of the indifference he had concerning his separation unto God. He was already blind spiritually before they gouged his eyes out. He finally awoke to his folly with his physical blindness helping him to see his foolishness. As his hair grew again, so did his reliance on God.

Having everything taken away that was once important was no longer an issue. His ministry was destroyed, his fame diminished. Yet in the midst of this, in his weakest and lowest moments, Samson was truly liberated from himself. He was liberated from the pride and selfishness that had plagued his life. His new focus was completely on God and what he could do to please the Master. Samson finally had the mentality that everything could be taken away from him, and that was okay, all that mattered was his relationship with God. The mockery of Jehovah by the people saddened him beyond measure, because he knew that he was the cause of such disrespect. So it goes without saying that his last prayer was one that didn't ask God to restore all that had been lost, instead it centered on destroying the enemies of God.

When we have lost the best that we could offer unto God in an evil day, our first thought is to hang it up and quit. We reason that if with our best we could not be successful in the Lord, then how can we think that without it we could continue on? If God had to depend on us giving Him our best, then He would be in a heap of trouble. The fact of the matter is this: God doesn't need our best for Him to accomplish His will. I can go a little further by saying that God doesn't even need us at all to accomplish His will.

Yet, there we are at an altar crying our eyes out, pleading with God to restore to us what has been lost. In all truth, if what we had lost was so important, God would have never allowed us to lose it in the first place. I believe that there's one attribute of God that we completely forget about. We can see Him as our Savior, Redeemer, Provider, and the like. What we don't realize about Him is that He continues to be a Creator.

My God is the only God that can create a universe from nothing. If this be so, and it is, then the little that we have left, given in faith, can produce miraculous results. Even when our best has been taken away, if we will give to Him what is left over, the outcome can be better than ever imagined. Why? GOD STILL USES WHAT IS LEFT OVER!

An Important Lesson Revisited

My evil day has now been prolonged for over four years. So much has been taken away, so much has been destroyed. The likelihood that I'll get it back grows dimmer as each day wears on. Because of my floundering faith, the Lord had to take me back several years before my evil day to re-teach me a lesson that I had forgotten.

The blows of life that have come my way have been somewhat damaging, crippling, and even devastating. There have been various times in my life when, after being pillaged by the devil, there has not been much left. It was after one of these blows that I started to feel sorry for myself. Instead of counting my blessings, I began to think about all that was wrong in my life. I started by how I saw myself physically. I know that I am one of the few surviving polio victims, and because of that, physically I am an oddball. Every time I extend my right hand to shake hands with someone, it confirms that fact. Some of the more polite people will take a sneak peek at my hand trying to figure out what is wrong without asking me personally. Then there are others that are not so polite that withdraw their hand shake, being repulsed by what they feel. They blurt out with a less than tactful, "What in the world happened to you?" I am constantly reminded of my oddity, every time I have to have pictures taken. The polio left me with my legs at different lengths, so when you look at me there is a Leaning Tower of Pisa effect. I always have to remember which way to lean to straighten myself out, so that the pictures can look normal. Clothes have never fit just right, because it's never easy to clothe a pear-shaped body. Losing my hair prematurely has never done anything for my self esteem, not to mention that what was left has grayed before its time. Socially, speaking only when I had to, many thought that perhaps I had a speech impediment or worse could not talk at all. That shaking hands business caused so much anxiety that I would shy away from people, especially after church services when shaking hands was expected. Finally, when God called me to become an evangelist, shortly after I had failed miserably in my one and only pastorate, I thought I was being mocked, because I knew I didn't have what it took to be a successful evangelist.

As all these thoughts swirled around in my head, making my life even more miserable, the Lord decided to make one of His unannounced visits. I wasn't in the mood to submit myself respectfully at a time when I was angry at Him for not keeping a promise. It was several years before that He had promised that my right arm would be healed, although to that day He still had not come through. I had been waiting patiently for Him, but for whatever reasons He thought it still was not the right time.

> "For I will restore health to you And heal you of your wounds," says the LORD, "Because they called you an outcast . . ."
>
> Jeremiah 30:17

God said, "Look at your left hand." "What about it?" I snapped. "I know that physically it is my strongest hand. It's the right one that I'm worried about."

The Lord always knows how to get His point across without making you feel as if you're being pushed. He gently continued by declaring that spiritually speaking my left hand was also my hand of strength. Then without intending to, He said something that made me feel so small. He said, "I don't use you because you're the greatest speaker that I could find. Neither do I use you for your eloquence as a teacher. The other abilities that you have used in my kingdom don't even come close to those of my other children. Nevertheless, there is a reason why I continue to call your name. You always seem to have oil in the palm of your left hand." He tenderly went on to say, "It could be in the wee hours of the morning when all others are asleep, yet when I call, you always come. Your thirst for my presence is one that is not found in most of my children, and it pleases me to no end every time you beckon to my call."

This reminder was made necessary because, during the evil day, my time with Him had diminished considerably. Time was not the only issue that eroded my trust in Him. His lack of affection while in His presence almost drove me to thoughts of suicide. As much as I had lost when I lost Gloria, it didn't come anywhere close to the misery and woe that I felt when it looked like He had given up on me. It is an ugly feeling to believe that God has turned His back on you. I can imagine now what people feel as they burn in hell without any hope. The despondency, despair, and the desolation that surrounds them as they suffer through an eternity without Christ would be more than any mind could possibly conceive.

Knowing that I had to humble myself once again wasn't as difficult as it had been in times past. With the freedom that I felt from forgiving Gloria under my belt, there was now nothing to stop me from pursuing His presence like I once had. It was like being born again, and although I would not like to return to that point in time in my relationship with Him, it sure beat where I had just come from. I never thought it my wildest imaginations that I could feel the presence of God as strongly as I do today. For such a long time, He removed His manifest presence, always believing that when it was all said and done, and the dust settled, I would still be there magnifying His holy name. I'm so glad He was right. It's all about the oil, the anointing that flows from the left hand to the right.

If the Lord were to come today where we are, asking us to extend our left hand out to Him, examining our palm to see

how much oil there was, how much would He find? Would
He find enough for us to get by, or would there be a handful
running over? It needn't matter, because whatever we need
God to be in our lives, that is what He will be. If at this point
in time our lives mirror the life of Samson, God is more than
willing to use what is left over. If our lives are more like that of
David, a constant visitor to the throne room of God, just let
the oil flow. Whatever the case may be, remember just one
thing, GOD STILL USES WHAT IS LEFT.

Chapter 8
I Will Not Settle

. . . I shall be satisfied when I awake in Your likeness.
Psalm 17:15

Satisfaction guaranteed! How many times have we been promised that, only to be a bit disappointed by their false claims? At least The Rolling Stones are truthful when they sing the song, "I Can't Get No Satisfaction." Webster defines *satisfaction* as "a fulfillment of a need or *desire.*" Strong's dictionary says that *to be satisfied* "to be full of." It is impossible to get any more you have finally come to the end of the road. To better understand what it means to be satisfied, it is only right to take Webster's definition and define the word *desire.* Webster's says that *desire,* as a noun, is "a conscious impulse toward something that promises enjoyment or satisfaction [there's that word again] in its attainment, whether good or bad." As a verb, it says, *desire* is "to long or hope for." When desires are not fulfilled, it's like opening a can of worms, because we accuse God of not being true to His Word.

> *Delight yourself also in the LORD, And He shall give*
> *you the desires of your heart.*
>
> Psalm 37:4

Have you ever delighted yourself in the Lord until it was coming out of your ears and still not had your desires granted? I have, and I have finally been able to understand why. What I thought were desires were nothing more than good intentions. "What's the difference?" you may ask. Good intentions are when we have something in mind as a goal. It never gets past the thinking stage. It sounds good, makes sense, and most of the time it's biblical, but until it has the opportunity to reach the heart, they are nothing more than good ideas. For example, a pastor comes excitedly to his congregation with a new direction for success. It includes a prayer and fasting chain that will commence on Monday. All that would like to participate in this program are asked to be at the church at 5 am. The response of the people is tremendous, shouting "Amen" throughout the whole sanctuary. At the time it sounds so good, and, of course, it makes sense, but come Monday morning no one shows up. The program intellectually moved them, but it never got to their heart.

What Causes Us to Settle

What happens when good intentions don't come to pass? We begin to rationalize our next step, lowering our expectations, and we settle. What exactly does it mean to settle? It means that we make an agreement to bring to a minimum the various differences in a particular situation. It happens all the time when a person settles his case out of court. The defendant will offer the plaintiff an enormous amount of money to go away and keep whatever would have been made public confidential. He is hoping that the amount will be big enough to persuade the plaintiff that it's not worth the trouble to go to court, waiting years for a judgment that would be based solely on principle. Most of the time the amount is too good to pass up, and a settlement is made.

Although both parties are not completely satisfied, an agreement is made that will come the closest to what both parties initially were asking for. It is the plaintiff, however, that must make the greatest sacrifices and compromises in order for the agreement to work. And there are very, very few people that I know that have enough integrity to stand for what is right, choosing instead a bundle of cash to satisfy their differences.

David knew the difference between desires and good intentions, being willing to put them under God's magnifying glass when he said:

> *Search me, O God, and know my heart: try me, and know my thoughts: And see if there be any wicked way in me, and lead me in the way everlasting.*
>
> Psalm 139:23-24

With his desires in check, knowing that they were directly from God, he could go on in his relentless pursuit of the presence of God. Why? Because he had a guarantee that God would satisfy his soul so completely that he wouldn't have to settle.

So glorious were the settings that God placed Adam in that it seemed preposterous that he would find himself in a situation where a decision had to be made to settle. When Adam decided to eat of the forbidden fruit, disobeying God's command, this is basically what he was willing to give up. His disobedience toward God meant that Adam would no longer have dominion of the entire Garden. Also affected was his intimate relationship with God, not to mention losing the glory of God that protected his innocence. We find ourselves asking, why was Adam willing to give up so much? I believe the answer is that living without his wife was unthinkable. We really don't know how long he lived in the garden without Eve, but he just couldn't bear the thought of living alone again. She had become the crowning moment of his existence, so he took a chance on the consequences of his sin.

Pride Rears Its Ugly Head

Pride will do that. It will constantly take a chance, because pride always breeds rebellion. Maybe he was banking on the fact that he was the only human being available to do God's will, and surely God would not destroy him. So he challenged the Word of God, and of course, he lost. His judgment consisted of a spiritual death that also had physical repercussions. As far as the woman was concerned, that excruciating pain she would have to endure in childbearing would be nothing in comparison to the fact that now her husband would rule over her.

The women of today have such a disdain for the teachings that God has left not only about leaving the man in charge of his family, but also that she as a wife must be subject to him. This is only part of a judgment that fell upon the woman for her disobedience. When God first created man and woman, the first name he gave them both was Adam (Gen. 5:2). It was His intention that together, side-by-side, they would rule the world. Adam, with the masculine traits of God, would rule with power, authority, and strength. Adam II (Eve) would rule with the tender characteristics of God: His love, patience, long-suffering, gentleness, etc. Together they would form the complete essence of God. All of that was lost through their disobedience; the woman was renamed, and from that day forward, her husband would rule over her. That is why the women of the world fight so viciously for equal rights, trying to regain the place that they lost when judgment fell in the Garden.

Adam also bore the harshness of God's judgment. The ground was cursed with thorns and thistles, and for the first time Adam would have to work for his food. The Garden of Eden would no longer be their home, meaning that they would have to leave the place where God and His glory reigned. Even the animals would become hostile, a new problem that would have to be reckoned with. Dying physically would have been much easier.

The reality of settling is that it's always worse than we can ever imagine. When we are put in a situation where we must lower our expectations, compromising one way or another to settle, our judgment is clouded by our emotions and we can't quite clearly see the ramifications of the decisions that we are about to make. That's why when we look at Adam's situation from a carnal point of view, we take his side, wondering what he had done wrong.

Wasn't Adam only doing what anyone else would have done? Wasn't he merely protecting what he loved the most? This is what I have been able to find out about God and what He requires of us in His service. At one time or another, we will have to put to death the love we have for our most treasured possession in this life.

Putting Everything on the Line

As harsh as that might appear, that is the exact situation that Abraham was put in. When he received his orders to kill his only son Isaac, it made no sense at all. Isaac was the answer to the promise that took twenty-five years to come to pass. If Isaac died, so did all the future blessings that were promised to Abraham's seed. The death of Isaac would mean that all of the hassle of being faithful to the promise of God during that time was completely in vain. Isaac's loss of life would imply that God was exactly like man and His word could not be trusted.

Unlike Adam, when Abraham's character was tested, it was faith, not pride, that came to the surface. Years ago, I heard T.F. Tenney say something about faith that I did not quite understand. He said, "Faith never dulls pain." Subsequently, I've learned that no matter how much faith you have in God, it does not lessen the pain that one will experience in the losses of life. Pain is no respecter of persons; it hits the faith-filled as hard as it hits the faithless. Regardless of the pain, a person filled with faith demonstrates that they will not settle. It is not in them to compromise, to lower their standard, or to leave God. They will believe God, even when they don't understand the terrors that have befallen them.

What is it that stopped God from allowing Abraham to kill Isaac? The obedience to His command is only part of it; what really caught God's attention was the fact that Abraham did it willingly. Abraham honestly believed that if he killed Isaac God would raise him from the dead. There is a scripture found in Hebrews that states:

> *Concluding that God was able to raise him up, even from the dead, from which he also received him in a figurative sense.*
>
> Hebrews 11:19

How did Abraham obtain that kind of faith? He did it by walking with God daily in intimate fellowship. Likewise, it is in His presence that we become more to God than just sons and daughters, we become friends. It's when our relationship with Him comes to that intimate level that He is more willing to share the secrets of life. Nothing is hidden, nor are the mysteries of God concealed. We are more readily prepared to take greater leaps of faith on what we don't understand, knowing that God will always come through regardless.

The Key to Success

The key to obtaining this kind of faith is found both in our willingness and obedience.

> *If you are willing and obedient, you shall eat the good of the land . . .*
>
> Isaiah 1:19

114

You can't have either/or for it to work the way God had ordained it originally. You must have both. I've known people that were so gung ho to do the work of God that their willingness to do anything greatly inspired others. When it came down to actually doing the job, however, it never got completed. It was their disobedience in the little things (showing up on time, paying tithes and offerings, respecting authority, etc.) that canceled out anything good that God wanted to accomplish in their lives. On the other hand, I've known others, who, like the Pharisees, obeyed even the most insignificant rules that were set before them. What denied them from eating the good of the land was the fact that everything was done with a spirit of griping. Nobody loves a whiner, including God. So if you don't have a right spirit while in His service, you might as well leave the job for someone else, because God is not going to accept your efforts anyway. If you are doing everything right because you have to and not because you want to, all of your efforts are in vain.

Obviously, the true test comes when we are willing to put everything on the line. That's God's way of testing our love for Him. There have been times, as I have searched the Scriptures, that I have come across some that I wish would have never been written. These are the kind of Scriptures that convict me of the things or ways in God that I have been found wanting. This next scripture is one of those:

> Yes, and all who desire to live godly in Christ
> Jesus will suffer persecution.
>
> 2 Timothy 3:12

The scripture emphatically says DESIRE, not good intentions. So many times I've heard Bible-believing Christians say that they serve God righteously without ever having to go through a bit of persecution. That worries me because, although their lives seem to measure up to the Word of God, the fact of the matter is a life without persecution goes against

Scripture. That is true for at least those who desire to live godly in Christ. Understand that because your desire to serve God is more than a good intention, all hell will break loose to make you change your mind.

Daniel's Audacity

Having to suffer did not stop Daniel. His prayer time with God was so important that he was willing to die for the privilege of being in the presence of God. Outwardly defiant, he opened his windows as he began to pray so that all could hear. I can now hear the *Santuchos* (Spanish slang for Pharisees) crying out that this is a bad idea. "Quit being so defiant, do you want to get yourself killed? You're not going to prove anything by being a martyr. Your premature death will be in vain, because there is no one to take your place have you thought about that?" Not surprisingly, he didn't listen to the naysayers and continued to pray. He was found out and then judged to die in the lions' den. If there ever was an opportunity for him to settle, for him to compromise his beliefs, for him to lower his standard, it was now. But when a man has close ties with God, settling is never an option. Let me tell you why.

The times spent alone with God bring a closeness to Him that is not found in every one of His children. The private conversations and the classified secrets that He is willing to share with us breed a confidence like no other. It is then that we can bind and loose things both in heaven and on earth, knowing that God will honor our word. The two greatest biblical examples of this can be found in the lives of Joshua and Elijah. When Joshua (Josh. 10:12-14) needed more time to defeat the enemies of God, he simply spoke the word in front of his entire army, and the sun stood still. This gave him the sufficient time needed to destroy his opponents. He did not receive these instructions from God; he was acting on his own and God honored his word.

> And there has been no day like that, before it or after it,
> that the LORD heeded the voice of a man; for the
> LORD fought for Israel.
>
> Joshua 10:14

God had the same type of confidence in Elijah. When he found himself in the presence of King Ahab, it was Elijah's words, not God's, that proclaimed that it would not rain in Israel for three years. Yet, the Lord honored these words, and it came to pass just as the prophet had decreed.

> And Elijah the Tishbite, of the inhabitants of
> Gilead, said to Ahab, "As the LORD God of Israel
> lives, before whom I stand, there shall not be dew nor
> rain these years, except at my word."
>
> 1 Kings 17:1

I believe that because Daniel had a similar relationship with God, the Lord took the time to warn him. Daniel was made privy to what was going to happen so that he could prepare himself in prayer. No one knows exactly what Daniel prayed when he went before the Lord three times a day. But somehow, I am inclined to accept that he was crying out for mercy in his supplications before it was needed. Whether he prayed a Psalm like this or not, I do not know, but it could have been something similar to this Psalm:

> The LORD has heard my supplication; The LORD will
> receive my prayer. Let all my enemies be ashamed and
> greatly troubled; Let them turn back and be ashamed
> suddenly.
>
> Psalm 6:9-10

Notice that when Daniel was put into the lions' den, there is no biblical record that he prayed. That is the difference between someone who has become intimate with God and everyone else, who waits till the tragedy strikes so that they can then go into heavy prayer and fasting. There is no need in trying times to fret or to pray in despair when you already know the outcome. That is one of the great benefits of our intimacy with Him. In the meantime, it was King Darius who was beside himself and took on the responsibility to knock on the doors of heaven in prayer and fasting, all night long. Can you imagine a heathen king crying out to a God that he does not know, believing that He will respond anyway? Well, he did, and it worked. When he woke up the next morning and hurried to see if Daniel was still alive, King Darius was ecstatic to hear Daniel's voice again.

Cruel to Be Kind?

For those of you that believe that God was so cruel to Daniel to be kind, consider a few things with me if you will. First of all, Daniel didn't feel that way, because again, he was told ahead of time what the outcome would be. Second of all, if the Lord would have allowed Daniel to pray in the lions' den, with the Lord responding to his plea, the effect of the miracle would not have been as dynamic. Let me explain. If Daniel prayed the prayer of deliverance, the publicity would go as far as the city gates. But God had greater things in mind in making His name known. Look at the effect that this miracle had on King Darius:

> *Then King Darius wrote: To all peoples, nations, and languages that dwell in all the earth: Peace be multiplied to you. I make a decree that in every dominion of my kingdom men must tremble and fear before the God of Daniel. For He is the living God, and steadfast forever; His kingdom is the one which shall not be destroyed, and His dominion shall endure to the end. He delivers and rescues, and He works signs and wonders in heaven and*

on earth, who has delivered Daniel from the power of the lions.

Daniel 6:25-27

If Daniel would have settled and stopped praying, the king would never have had the opportunity to go one-on-one with the Lord. It was this life-changing experience that moved him to write his decree to the entire world. Now everyone, not just those within the city gates, would know that Jehovah was God Almighty and there was no God like Him. Although Daniel, perhaps, did not know specifically how the outcome was going to be, he had enough confidence in his God to stand for what was right, not to settle in any way, knowing that God was going to work things out perfectly.

A Final Look at Psalm 17:15

Except for in the beginning of the chapter, we really haven't touched on the scripture in Psalms 17:15. In all honesty, we will never awake in His likeness, until after the rapture, of course. If this be true, then why even try? The fact that we struggle and strain and strive to be conformed to the image of Christ shows to Him that we haven't yet reached that satisfaction stage, the one where we begin to settle for other things apart from God. What we are demonstrating to Him after all these years is that there's still a longing to be in His presence and that nothing shall separate us from the love of Christ. Is that how you feel? Or have you settled? Have the difficulties of life caused you to compromise your beliefs one way or another? The pains of the cross can be difficult to bear; that's why so many backslide and go back to the world. But in reality, it's God's only way to Him.

> Then Jesus said to His disciples, "If anyone desires to come after Me, let him deny himself, and take up his cross, and follow Me."

Matthew 16:24

There's that word again, *desire*. It seems to be the word that separates the men from the boys. We all want to do good for God. All of us have good intentions, but good intentions are not good enough. The Word of God has not changed over the years. If we are to follow Him in His pathway, then we are going to have to deny ourselves of some things. In today's world of indulgence, denying yourself is not an option. It truly boils down to what you desire, anything less would be SETTLING.

An evil day has its way of making even the strongest people of God crumble to their knees and woefully settle. I can't say that I'm such a strong man in God, neither can I admit that I am wiser than most. All I know is that throughout this whole ordeal, God has been faithful and it has been His grace that has kept me. Because of it, I have made this promise to Him that no matter what comes my way in the future, I WILL NOT SETTLE.

Chapter 9
Think on These Things

Finally, brethren, whatsoever things are true, whatsoever things are honest, whatsoever things are just, whatsoever things are pure, whatsoever things are lovely, whatsoever things are of good report; if there be any virtue, and if there be any praise, think on these things

Philippians 4:8

Thinking clearly during an evil day is perhaps one of the most difficult things that will ever be asked of you. All that you do, all that you say, and all that you think is in such a chaotic mess that solving the most uncomplicated problems becomes a most strenuous challenge. By definition, when we think we take time to weigh something mentally, taking a mental inventory that will not only take time, but will usually be somewhat arduous.

We would prefer to reserve this kind of job for the meticulous, the bean counters of society that have nothing better to do than waste an entire day thinking. We would rather do things without thinking, you know, just shooting from the hip with no nerves involved and just dealing with the losses later. When we choose to deal with things in that fashion, we get away with a lot. The downside is that many times the damage is irreversible.

How God Thinks About Us

Not surprisingly, the Lord is our best example that even He the King of Kings takes time to think, so that when adverse situations arise He will not react to them unfavorably. When the Lord thinks about us, His thoughts are always good thoughts.

> *For I know the thoughts that I think toward you, says the LORD, thoughts of peace and not of evil, to give you a future and a hope.*
> Jeremiah 29:11

Even when he chastens (trains) us, love is at the center of every thought.

> *For whom the LORD loves He corrects, Just as a father the son in whom he delights.*
> Proverbs 3:12

It behooves us to follow in His footsteps having the "mind of Christ," thinking like He thinks, so that we can get through an evil day.

In a prior chapter I mentioned that it was pretty much impossible to explain step-by-step how I got through my evil day. Because the grace of God took complete control of my situation, many times I found myself on autopilot. However, there is a train of thought that the Lord would want us to undertake that will help us even under the most undesirable conditions and bears looking into.

When the apostle Paul wrote Philippians 4:8, because he was such a scholar, I thought that he was bunching adjectives together to impress those that he was writing to. Little did I know that the order in which these adjectives were being placed was a pattern for success that the apostle wanted all to follow.

Whatsoever Is True

He begins with whatsoever things are true. He uses the Greek word ALETHES, which means "unconcealed truth." If we are truly to obtain the mind of Christ, then our thoughts every day must begin with God Himself. The hidden God of the Old Testament is now completely revealed in the New Testament. When the veil in the temple rent in two after Jesus died on Calvary, all that was concealed about God was brought out into the open, to whosoever will. This truth should be our focal point as we begin our day. The best way to do this, I have found, is in early morning prayer. I know that all of us have different schedules and preferences as to when we come to the throne of God. Our daily devotion is predicated on what's best for us, so that we can make time for the Master. But look at the words David wrote about seeking God early:

> O God, You are my God; Early will I seek You; My soul thirsts for You; My flesh longs for You In a dry and thirsty land Where there is no water. So I have looked for You in the sanctuary, To see Your power and Your glory.
> Psalm 63:1-2

In my experiences as an evangelist traveling throughout the country, there was one thing in common that I found amongst the churches that were growing like gangbusters. Most of them had early morning prayer programs, while the most successful prayed 24/7. I was never more impressed than I was when I got to visit a church in Colorado Springs. Their auxiliary building included a bookstore, a chapel which was bigger than most local church buildings, and a boatload of prayer rooms. As I looked on the wall to see the names of those that were praying at various hours, I thought that when it came to the early morning hours, the list would diminish. Much to my surprise, the list was pretty much the same, if not more so. I thought about the success that church had, and I came to the conclusion that because there were people willing to seek God early in the sanctuary, God truly was responding. I pretty much understand that it is not mandatory to come to the house of God to pray, but there is something about getting a hold of the hand of God in the early part of the day, with the brethren, that just makes your day that much better. David said it this way: "I thirst and long to see your power and your glory in your sanctuary" (paraphrase of Psalm 63:1-2). To do this daily is probably one of the greatest advantages that we as Christians can have.

Whatsoever Is Honest

We move onto the next category, which is thinking on whatsoever is honest. The Greek word used here, *SEMNOS*, means "honorable, worthy of being honored." It's not so much whatsoever, but now it also includes whosoever. We move from whom we can't see, God, to whom we can see, people. Isn't it amazing how our loved ones are usually the ones that are dishonored the most? We can go through the day having to deal with a grouchy boss, taking all the garbage that he dishes out, and then we come home we take it out on anything and everything in sight. We kick the dog, we whack the kids, and we yell at the wife . . . no one is safe. In spite of that, we are told by the Word of God to give honor to whom honor is due.

Honor all people.

1 Peter 2:17

Peter's words are so simple, yet still out of reach when we have to include the people closest to us. What that means then is that we must make a conscious effort to include them in our honoring of people. In other words, we must THINK. How do we do that? By attaching high value to them; that's exactly what we are doing when we honor them. This can be accomplished by making them feel secure, verbally praising them, and finally protecting them from fears and from other people. When we get the hang of it, then we are ready to go to the next step.

Whatsoever Is Just

Now we can think about those things that are just. By definition the apostle is telling us that it's time to think about keeping His commandments. Our focus moves from people back to the Word of God.

Your word I have hidden in my heart, That I might not sin against You.

Psalm 119:11

It was David's intention to make sure that the Word of God found a lodging place in his heart. He knew that once it was there, he would be tough to beat. He wanted to be certain that what he was feeling from God was truly desires, and not good intentions. Once he allowed these desires to capture his heart, he would then do this:

Keep your heart with all diligence, For out of it spring the issues of life.

Proverbs 4:23

He understood that from your heart comes your source for living. What is your source? Is it godly or ungodly? When we think about the things that we do daily, from what source do we pull? Are the Scriptures the source that we run to, or are our thoughts dominated by what we read in the newspaper and watch on the news? The Word of God is not only trustworthy, but keeping God's commandments brings blessing. Our obedience to His Word is the source of our blessing.

> *The blessing, if you obey the commandments of the LORD your God which I command you today; and the curse, if you do not obey the commandments of the LORD your God . . .*
>
> Deuteronomy 11:27-28

What are the benefits that blessing will bring to our life? The Scriptures tell us that blessings bring righteousness (Ps. 24:5) and life (Ps. 133:3). When God blesses His people, it will bring prosperity (2 Sam. 7:29) and salvation (Ps. 3:8). Whatever good God has to shower upon His people, it comes when His commandments are obeyed.

Whatsoever Is Pure

It has taken three categories of thinking to finally get to the place where we think about ourselves. In this fourth category, where we think about those things that are pure, the Lord wants our thoughts to be pure from carnality, to be chaste, and to be modest. That means that we move from thinking about God's commands so that we can look inward to ourselves. The battle with carnality is never conquered; it can only be controlled. Our convictions, beliefs, and truths are compromised when the carnal mind is in control. Haven't you ever noticed that when a person backslides, he always goes back to what once controlled his life as a sinner? If he was once an alcoholic, then he will run back to the bottle. If it was drugs that had him bound, then he will go desperately looking for his next fix. It really doesn't matter what it was, because as the Scriptures say:

> *As a dog returns to his own vomit, So a fool repeats his folly.*

> Proverbs 26:11

We have to make the greatest of efforts to keep our thoughts pure, because once the carnal mind is in control, it fights against God.

> *For to be carnally minded is death, but to be spiritually minded is life and peace. Because the carnal mind is enmity against God; for it is not subject to the law of God, nor indeed can be. So then, those who are in the flesh cannot please God.*

> Romans 8:6-8

The carnal mind is so putrid in the eyes of God that it becomes His enemy. Why would we ever want to get on God's bad side? What's even worse is that when we are carnally minded, we can never be pleasing to Him. Pleasing God is what we should always live for. When our minds are pure from carnality, that is what creates the holiness in our lives that God longs for. Remember His words to us:

> *Be holy, for I am holy.*

> 1 Peter 1:16

Thinking pure thoughts will cleanse our minds continuously, a process that is needful if we are ever to be pleasing to Him.

Whatsoever Is Lovely

Now we can move on to a category that most young men do automatically. The apostle goes on to tell us that we must think about those things that are lovely. Sadly to say, young men, it's not what you think. When Paul wrote this, he meant for us to think about those things that are acceptable and pleasing in the eyes of others. That means that we are to think about things that we can do, say, and be, so that others can follow in our footsteps. Passing on good things to the next generation should be a requirement, not an option. Whether you realize it or not, there is someone who is always watching you. For whatever reasons they idolize you, so much so that they will copy everything that you do, down to your freaky hairdo and your funky way of dress. They say that imitation is the greatest form of flattery, and if that be so, they are not only imitating your good, but also your bad. So you need to take some time to think about things that will positively affect those that someday will follow in your footsteps. Don't worry about giving too much, because you can never give too much. Giving to others above and beyond the call of duty only invokes another scripture of blessing:

> *There is one who scatters, yet increases more; And there is one who withholds more than is right, But it leads to poverty.*
>
> Proverbs 11:24

The Lord's ways are always so different than our ways, but if we can remember that freely we have received, that we will freely give.

A Good Report

The final process in our thinking deals with things that will show a good report. In this category, Paul wanted us to think about those well-spoken-of things about ourselves. In other words, the apostle wanted us to take some time to look at our reputation, which is our most prized possession. Once your reputation is lost, it is very, very difficult to regain. I would like to say this to the females who are reading this book. As unfair as it might seem, we live in a male dominated world. The rules are set to favor men. Sadly to say, when a man goes out and parties with a lot of different women, it is considered him just being a man. On the other hand, when a woman does the same thing, she is considered a floozy. If a man cannot hold his liquor, he is said to be the life of the party. But if a woman drinks too much, she is labeled a lush. Be it as it may, a woman has to try doubly hard to make sure that her reputation is not tainted in any way. The effort is worth the trouble, because if you happen to blemish your reputation in any way, it will come back to haunt you for the rest of your life. I have seen ministries, relationships, reputations, even lives that have been lost when, in a moment of temptation, the consequences of sin had not been well thought out. God always forgives, but people aren't that kind.

> *Do not be deceived, God is not mocked; for whatever a man sows, that he will also reap.*
> Galatians 6:7

When Paul wrote this scripture to the Galatians, it was not his intention to strike fear in the children of God. Although God will allow a man's doings to run its course, sometimes in tragic consequences, the sowing and reaping principle has more to do with man than it does with God. You see, whenever we sin and repent of that sin, we can then ask God for forgiveness, and He is there immediately to do so. At that moment He not only forgives but He forgets.

The reason why the problem still lingers, after God has already forgotten about it, is that we still have to deal with people. People will say to our face that they have forgiven us; but unlike God, they do not forget. When sin comes into the life of a child of God and is forgiven, the reason they stop serving Him, more times than not, is because the people in the church won't let it die. That is what Paul meant when he said that we would reap what we sow. If there was ever a part of our life that we needed to consider thinking more about, it is our reputation.

Virtue and Praise

We have come to the point in the Scripture where Paul warns us with a big "if." The virtue and praise part of the Scripture, if not included in the categories that we have been thinking about, will negate the whole process. It has to be clear that both tests must be passed. Either/or just doesn't cut it. How could any of the things that Paul has admonished us to think about not have any virtue or praise? The tests can and do fail when it's not the right time. For God, ultimately, timing is everything.

When God gave me a word for a beautiful young lady that He wanted me to minister to, I didn't have the courage to tell her, because His Word seemed so far out of whack. She was not only beautiful, she was drop-dead gorgeous. His message to her was that, although she had been living in a lesbian relationship, if she was willing to repent, God would forgive her and take her back into the fold. At that time being so new to the gifts of the Spirit, I thought it best just to leave it alone, because it probably wasn't God anyway. The next service I did what God had asked, but the timing was wrong. She didn't believe the message because she thought that I had talked to her brother, who at that time was in our rehabilitation program. The mercy of God is so great that, even when we mess up, He can fix things so that He can get the glory. Knowing that we would have to approach this from a different direction, He then told me to ask her who Maria was. When I did, with a terrified look on her face, she began to cry. No one, and I mean no one, knew that Maria was her new lover. It was only then that she knew that God still cared for her and wanted her back. If we are to be successful in God, we must be willing to try the thoughts that we are thinking, so that if there be any virtue and praise, God can get all the glory.

When we have successfully completed the process that the apostle has set before us, our thoughts should move more into the direction of meditation. When we meditate, we reckon inward, counting up or weighing the reasons why we should do so. We take on the face of a jury that must deliberate to find the correct verdict. Why such a strong admonition? The reason is this: adulthood has dulled our positivism. As adults we seem to find the worst in every thing. No wonder Jesus says that unless we become as little children, we cannot enter into the kingdom of heaven (Matt. 18:3).

Out of the Mouths of Babes

Years ago, while I was working at a particular Christian school, one of the younger students was tragically killed in an auto accident. He was not wearing a seat belt, and upon impact, he flew from the back seat toward the front, crashing his head against the windshield. The force of the collision was so great that his head broke through the windshield and the broken glass decapitated him. His parents were not saved at the time, and they took it extremely hard.

During the funeral service, I had some time to meditate on Steven and some experiences that my family and I had had with him. He was a rambunctious little guy, a bundle of energy. My oldest daughter and he were in the same kindergarten class. It was not uncommon to see him at recess running around the playground chasing the girls, especially my Stephanie. He was so full of life that he would light up any room that he would walk into. When the day of graduating the kindergarten class came, I remember him walking down the aisle with the biggest smile on his face. So radiating was his pride that you knew that he had accomplished something special.

As a parent, all I could think about was how I would have reacted if the same thing would have happened to any of my children. Accidents like this never make any sense, especially when it happens to little ones. It was never meant for a parent to have to bury their children. Being adults as well as being parents, this loss hit us all pretty hard. On the way home from the funeral service, my wife and I continued the conversation of the tragedy that we had just experienced. We kept on harping on his death, and the more we thought about it the more morbid the conversation got. In the mean time in the backseat, there was a completely different conversation going on.

My children were not talking about how Steven died, they were talking about how he lived. With all of the laughing that was going on back there, it was hard to believe that we were all talking about the same person. Stephanie, of course, was dominating the conversation, because she knew Steven the best. With much gusto, she would recount her playground experiences, and I could swear that tomorrow when her class was let out for recess, Steven would be chasing her again. The Lord spoke to me and said, "Listen to your children and how they express their thoughts. They don't dwell on the bad, only on the good. That's how I would want you to think as you go on in your everyday life."

Thinking of the things that the apostle has written to us will always bring life, no matter what comes our way. Evil day or not, our thoughts can always bring Him the glory that He deserves. What will you choose to think on?

Chapter 10
Remember Elder Ross

And if it seems evil to you to serve the LORD, choose for yourselves this day whom you will serve . .

.Joshua 24:15

Decisions, decisions, decisions! We make them all the time, usually without putting much thought to them. When we wake up in the morning, we must decide which foot we will use to step out of bed. Then we decide whether it will be the left or right slipper that we put on first. And so on and so forth, we make decisions like these throughout the entire day. Most of the decisions that we will make are ones that don't take thought, because they are the same ones that we have continually made for years. The more difficult decisions we have to deal with are the ones that come with less frequency and carry more weight. It's one thing to decide what you're going to have for breakfast, it's another thing to know who you're going to choose to marry and spend the rest of your life with. What makes these decisions even more stressful is when we feel that our choices are limited. When our options are great, then there's really no pressure to make a wrong decision. It's when we are up against the wall, with limited resources available to us and the clock is ticking, that we freak out, knowing that a wrong decision could change the course of our entire life. It is usually then in our fear of making a wrong decision that we become paralyzed, not wanting to choose at all. When we get to that point, there's only so much that God can do. Knowing that a decision can be made only when a choice is made, God encourages us to choose. No matter what has befallen us in the cares of life, God knows without a shadow of a doubt that we can always choose Him and all of the wonderful benefits that come with serving Him. We in turn can know that we have made the right choice, because deciding to live for God is always the right decision.

A Sobering Thought

I have begun this chapter talking about choices and decisions for one reason. In the aftermath of the most grueling experiences that I have had to endure in my entire lifetime, decision-making, even in the most simple situations, had become difficult. I have come to the realization that, although God has healed me of many ill feelings, destructive thoughts, and sinful emotions, the complete repairing of my heart is going to take some time. Of course, believing that God could repair it in an instant would be wishful thinking, because in matters of the heart, God always uses time. It's only when a heart has been hardened with bitterness that God cannot get through. It is then that God must crush the heart and recreate it once again. But as long as a heart stays tender, God can do what He does best, and that is to bring us back to complete health.

When we look at the life of Christ here on earth, we completely misconstrue the reasons why He was ultimately victorious. Because of His deity, we downplay the severity of the pain that He actually endured. Because He was a God Man, perfect in every way, we picture Him as a physically strong, uncharacteristically handsome, debonair man, who waltzed through life without any problem. Look how Isaiah describes this healer from Galilee:

> *For He shall grow up before Him as a tender plant, And as a root out of dry ground. He has no form or comeliness; And when we see Him, There is no beauty that we should desire Him. He is despised and rejected by men, A Man of sorrows and acquainted with grief. And we hid, as it were, our faces from Him; He was despised, and we did not esteem Him.*
>
> Isaiah 53:2-3

We expected royalty because of His lineage. He was to be the son of David. In turn we got a Son of a poor carpenter. We expected His entry with pomp and circumstance. In turn we got a quiet Man, one that was inconspicuous to His surroundings. We expected a handsome, charming Man, much like Moses or David, who were of a beautiful countenance. In turn we got a Man that shows no beauty that we might desire Him. We expected Him to live a life of ease and leisure. In turn we got a Man that did not even have a place to rest His head. We expected a dynamic personality, one that would overwhelm you. In turn we got a Man of sorrows acquainted with grief. So much so that we could honestly say that grief was His most intimate acquaintance.

Enduring the Worst

What actually did He have to endure? He endured sorrows that bruised Him. When the subject of His name came up, all manner of evil was said against Him. Hardly any man could

135

endure the wounds and stripes that were given Him from being scourged. He was wronged and abused, judged for something He did not deserve. Being afflicted both in mind and body, oppressed beyond end, He did not break. He knew that His persecutors hated Him because they honestly believed that God also hated Him; this certainly weighed heavy on His mind. The scripture in Hebrews adequately describes what He endured:

> *But was in all points tempted as we are, yet without sin.*
> Hebrews 4:15

The passage of time makes it far easier to paint a different picture than what the Scriptures tell us. It also makes it much easier to rationalize our failure to follow in His footsteps. The fact of the matter is this: there is one and only one reason why He, Jesus, was able to endure all that He did. And it has nothing to do with His deity. He was able to bear such pain because never once in His adversity did He harden His heart:

> *For He shall grow up before Him as a tender plant . . .*
> Isaiah 53:2

From Bethlehem to Calvary, His heart always stood within the boundaries of this scripture. He not only grew in stature and in grace, but also in tenderness of heart. He understood the blessings of a tender heart, ones that we push away so readily, because the disadvantages far outweigh the benefits. The greatest benefit of a tender heart, although it can be easily wounded and taken advantage of, is that it can never, ever, ever be broken. Let me tell you why. It's pretty much like a tender piece of meat. Bang it as much as you will with a hammer. Unless it has been exposed to the air and other elements, the most that you will get out of your efforts is a badly bruised piece of meat. In similar fashion, a tender heart is one that is filled with forgiveness. It is a spirit of forgiveness that helps keep bitterness completely out. Why is this so important?

Because when bitterness settles in a heart, not even God can penetrate it; it has to be broken then recreated to bring honor to God. King David under stood this principle when he pleaded with the Lord to create a new heart within:

> *Create in me a clean heart, O God, And renew a steadfast spirit within me.*
>
> Psalm 51:10

This petition before God came after the prophet Nathan exposed his sin. After a period of deep reflection, David came to the conclusion that his heart was not repairable. So hardened was his heart that even the most base things became common in his everyday life, not even giving them a second thought. Is it any wonder that David began to plead with God about a situation that he himself could not control?

Perhaps the greatest advantage of having a tender heart is that, when it is hurt, it can mend itself.

> *Therefore, having these promises, beloved, let us cleanse ourselves from all filthiness of the flesh and spirit, perfecting holiness in the fear of God.*
>
> 2 Corinthians 7:1

This is possible because a saint of God with a tender heart will always take the first step to humble himself. In his humility, he is able to put blame aside, which in turn makes fault a non-issue. So many tragedies, lawsuits, divorces, and the like could be avoided, if only blame and fault could be thrown out the window. Once we get to the point in our lives that we can accept whatever comes our way regardless of fault, then the Lord can sweep on in and do His thing.

> *God resists the proud, but gives grace to the humble.*
>
> James 4:6

137

The Pride of Absalom

If only Absalom, David's son, could have taken the hint. His heart began to harden when he allowed envy to seep in. He was tired of hearing about how great his father was. In his eyes he was as good-looking, just as intelligent, equally as strong if not more so, and wise beyond his years. His envy begat pride and impatience. It was then that bitterness began to rear its ugly head, and all hell broke loose. With a heart hardening more and more by the minute, Absalom proclaimed himself to be the king of Israel before his time. David's love for him was so great that he would have gladly given him the throne, if only asked. But nobody could talk sense to Absalom. Why? Because this wayward son had hardened his heart. As a result of his actions, Absalom ran away, not only from his pursuers, but also from the presence of God.

While on the run, Absalom's hair was caught in the thick bough of an oak tree, and he was left there hanging. As Joab (one of David's men) found him completely exposed and helpless, he pierced his heart with his deadly darts, killing him on the spot. Just a few more years and the throne would have been rightfully his. A hardened heart not only cost Absalom his inheritance, it cost him his life. When you harden your heart, it will always leave you hanging without a leg to stand on. You will be left unprotected, and Satan will go directly to the heart to steal what God has promised.

A Chink in the Armor

At the height of an evil day, because of the frequency and the intensity of the attacks, a heart begins to harden many times without even knowing it. Sadly to say, what most people don't realize is that an overabundant amount of blessing can have the same effect. I learned something about Job that I had never before seen in his life. It was pride that turned out to be the chink in his armor. And it was this character fault that God used to bait Satan into tormenting him relentlessly. The Lord needed to soften his heart, because prosperity brought a hardness that ultimately would destroy him. The fault is so well disguised and so deeply hidden from Job that it's difficult to grasp that this a big reason why God allowed Satan to come and wreak havoc in his life.

Job's pride is evident in his daily prayer for his children. Although he was doing what God would want every God-fearing parent to do, he was doing it for the wrong reasons.

> *And his sons would go and feast in their houses, each on his appointed day, and would send and invite their three sisters to eat and drink with them. So it was, when the days off easting had run their course, that Job would send and sanctify them, and he would rise early in the morning and offer burnt offerings according to the number of them all. For Job said, "It may be that my sons have sinned and cursed God in their hearts." Thus Job did regularly.*
>
> Job 1:4-5

Instead of teaching his children how to pray so that they could form a relationship for themselves, he took it upon himself to cover all the bases with his own personal prayer. He knew that God would never say no to him, so he felt more comfortable doing it his way. It's the same thing that happens when we as parents don't want to take the time to train our children to do their chores. We know that they can't make their bed or wash the dishes or cut the lawn as well as we can, so instead of taking extra time to help them get to a place of competency, we just do it ourselves. What Job's prayers were actually demonstrating was his impatience to do the right thing. His people skills were less than perfect and, in the case of his children, were completely found wanting.

There was a man in the land of Uz, whose name was Job; and that man was blameless and upright, and one who feared God and shunned evil.

Job 1:1

The King James Version uses the word *perfect* instead of "blameless." I believe because of our perception that he was absolutely perfect, what I have mentioned above is somewhat unbelievable. If he was perfect or even blameless, how could I come to the conclusion that Job had a defect that only God could see? I took the time to look up the definition of the word *perfect* in the King James Version, and I found out that it literally means "to be pious," a word that is used to show reverence to God. His reverence to the Lord was impeccable, that's why when he lost everything; his animals, his servants, his own children, he doesn't blame God.

Then Job arose, tore his robe, and shaved his head; and he fell to the ground and worshiped. And he said: "Naked I came from my mother's womb, and naked shall I return there. The LORD gave, and the LORD has taken away; blessed be the name of the LORD." In all this Job did not sin nor charge God with wrong.

Job 1:20-22

His dealing with people, on the other hand, left something to be desired. A man that has never experienced suffering has intolerance for people who are. He believes that they have brought it upon themselves, and using his own life as an example makes proof that what he's saying is true. There is no mercy or compassion, and he is quick to judge. And although he has the ability to help in whatever way that is needed to get them out of their turmoil, he refuses because he feels that God is just teaching them a lesson. I don't think that what I believe about Job is too far-fetched. Haven't you ever in your Christian experience come across somebody that was a great worshipper?

One who seems to do everything right in God? You know the ones that I'm talking about. From a distance they inspire us to touch God the way they do. We try to pattern our lives exactly like theirs, mimicking their every move, until we meet them personally. We then find out that because we don't seem to be at their level of spirituality, they won't even give us the time of day. Looking down on us the entire time, we leave them with a bitter taste in our mouth. That was Job.

I too fell into this trap at the height of God using me miraculously. If people did not follow the program while I was ministering, more times than not I would just ignore them. When questioned about my methods of ministry (sometimes they are quite bizarre), I was offended by their audacity. Who were they to tell me what was right and what was wrong? I was the one that the Spirit of God was flowing through, not them. So I took them as personal attacks, ones that were forcefully directed at me to bring me down. I had pretty much taken on a me-versus-the-world mentality, because I was one of the first in our organization to be used by God in such a way. It is amazing what an evil day can do to one's pride. As Satan was allowed to buffet me from every angle possible, my despair in trying to find help only increased my awareness of the pain most people were suffering. For the first time I truly understood why people waiting for prayer were so anxious for me to pick them out of the crowd and minister to their various needs. My approach of ministering is somewhat unique, in that it's mostly one-on-one. Because I deal with only those that God has individually handpicked, it takes an enormous amount of time. I understand that forming lines to deal with all the needs is pretty much the status quo and initially that is what I did. But after years of experiencing more people not receiving from God than those that did, I changed my method. I may not be able to reach the masses in this fashion, because of time constraints, but then again whoever God does send me to always receive their answer.

When all the dust had settled, and the lessons that God needed to teach Job were complete, his words and attitude changed.

> *I have heard of You by the hearing of the ear, but now my eye sees You. Therefore I abhor myself, and repent in dust and ashes.*
>
> Job 42:5-6

Job's New Perception of God

As blessed as this man of God was, his view of the Lord was completely distorted. He only knew the God of prosperity. Up until the time of his evil day, he had only heard about the various ways that God provided for his other children. But coming away from the most painful experience a man could bear without dying, his view of God drastically changed. Through his ordeal he began to become acquainted with the God of consolation. His sorrows brought him face-to-face with the God of compassion. His personal losses, the greatest being the loss of his children, had allowed him to come in contact with the God of restoration.

When the nightmare grew the darkest and his wife rebuked him to curse God and die, the God of peace in the midst of the storm quietly calmed his troubled soul. So many attributes of God that had been hidden because of so much blessing, how could Job know that God had an abundant supply of them that he was not even aware of? His new perception of God, with a tender heart once again in place, allowed him to humble himself before the presence of God.

> *Therefore I abhor myself, and repent in dust and ashes.*
>
> Job 42:6

Coming full circle, realizing what was wrong in his life with the willingness to change, he began his restoration period at ground zero. There's not much detail as to the process he underwent to get back at the level of prosperity that he was at before his evil day. Yet through the Scriptures, I have a good idea what his experience was like, one similar to mine.

> *But those who wait on the LORD Shall renew their strength; They shall mount up with wings like eagles, They shall run and not be weary, They shall walk and not faint.*
>
> Isaiah 40:31

The restoration period for one who has experienced an evil day will be one that falls into the category of renewing one's strength by walking. I know that the scripture mentions that it's possible to mount up with wings like eagles, and I know that we as Pentecostals love to fly. Of course, if that's not possible, there's nothing wrong with running, especially having the ability to run all day long without being weary. But the last portion of the scripture is one that we do not take a liking to. Walking in our eyes is reserved for the crippled, the elderly, or the newborn in Christ. It is what is done in God when you can't do anything else. But the Lord in His wisdom understood what an evil day was all about. And because pretty much all of your strengths, talents, gifts, possessions, relationships, and the like had been either somewhat damaged or completely destroyed, your resistance to opposition is very, very low. Although God is with us every step of the way, we find ourselves stumbling over even the most trivial of things. It will take a lot of time and patience for us to get back to where we have been. The temptation to want to run and fly will always be in the back of our minds.

Physically, this year has been the most taxing. Having to deal with the after effects of polio all my life, there have been many things that I have been restricted in doing. Because of that, my ability to jog (I'm too slow to run) is something that I have cherished most highly. But this year has been different. Various pains have racked my body, including pains in my legs.

143

After various tests, the doctors still aren't sure what is causing my right leg to lose muscle mass. It could be anything from neuropathy caused by my diabetes to post polio syndrome, which seems to be the disease coming back to the body after being dormant for many years. I can't run stairs at this time; neither can I jog, which I had been doing for over thirty years. The doctors have encouraged me to walk. Oh, how I hate to walk. It's so boring, and to tell you the truth, at this time with the pains in my legs it seems to hurt even more than when I jogged.

Spiritual Comparisons

I believe that the Lord is only paralleling physically the restoration process that He is trying to accomplish spiritually. Walking with the Lord daily at times can be boring. Processing everything that comes my way falls into the category of humdrum. As I have tried to force myself to run both spiritually and physically, there is a lot of falling down. The Lord finally had to help me understand what he was doing in my life to help me avoid hurting myself during this time of waiting, keeping it to a walk.

> But may the God of all grace, who called us to His eternal glory by Christ Jesus, after you have suffered a while, perfect, establish, strengthen, and settle you.
> 1 Peter 5:10

This whole process of perfecting, establishing, strengthening, and settling can only begin after we have suffered a while. The Lord knows that after a period of suffering, with the right attitude, great things can be created. It is sad to think that, as with many things as God is, we rarely see Him as a Creator. More important is the fact that He is a re-creator in our lives. It is His way of taking a bad, negative situation and turning it around completely. He then can give us a blessing that we will not even be able to contain. But He chooses long, extended periods of time to mold us pretty much the same way a good cook prepares a delicious meal.

The Process Begins

He begins with perfecting. It's nothing like it sounds, because our lives will not become absolutely perfect. What God actually does for us is that He completely and thoroughly repairs, mends, and restores our lives. We can count on His perfect ways to make all the wrong in our life right. It's all about Him, not us. When Moses received his call from God, he immediately showed his carnality. He not only moved before its time, he tried to solve a spiritual problem in a physical way. Relying on his Egyptian upbringing and know-how, it only worsened the problem and he was forced to run away. He played into God's hands in that in the desert away from any Egyptian influence, God had an opportunity to repair, mend, and restore him.(Ex. 2,3) The lessons that he learned after forty years of silence are not revealed to us in Scripture. I believe that they are too personal, yet have a profound effect, so much so that there is a complete change in his life. They undo his worldly mindset so that he can think like God.

The next stage that the Lord begins to deal with in our lives is one that will establish us. To be *established,* according to Strong's dictionary, is "to turn in a certain, distinct direction." Of course it is God that points us in the right direction, promising to guide us to the end of our destination. Not even our shortcomings, failures, or faults can stop the power of God from succeeding, because it is in our weakness that we are made strong. Moses was quite apprehensive to respond to God's call, because in his eyes he was not good enough.

Surely the inability to speak was grounds enough to deny him into the fraternity of the mightily used. The problem was that God was not looking for perfection, only for his best effort. Even when our best effort is not good enough, God knows how to make up the difference by the power of His Spirit.

The apostle Paul could identify with Moses in that, because he didn't walk with Jesus when he was alive, and so he felt unqualified to be called an apostle. So the Lord evened things up by hiding Paul in the desert, and what he doesn't know through personal experience God opened his understanding in personal revelation. Paul was now ready to be pointed in the right direction, with nothing to stop him.

When Moses accepted his weaknesses, he too began to believe that God would make up the difference. The Lord had the opportunity to point him back toward Egypt to rescue his people.

The process continues when we are strengthened by God. Again by definition, Strong says that when we are strengthened by Him, it means that we are confirmed by spiritual knowledge and power. There is a great difference between being pointed in the right direction and demonstrating power in God. When the call of God came to Moses, the Lord asked of him to use only what he already had, his rod and staff. How could shepherding tools be effective against the most powerful king of the world? Place anything in the hands of God and watch Him annihilate the competition.

> *But God has chosen the foolish things of the world to put to shame the wise, and God has chosen the weak things of the world to put to shame the things which are mighty . . . that no flesh should glory in His presence.*
> 1 Corinthians 1:27,29

Once Moses trusted God through his obedience, the power of God was unleashed, confirming his call through signs and wonders. God always honors faith. It is faith that moves heaven not need. But Satan will always give a good fight. Because Satan never goes down easily, he used Pharaoh's wizards to duplicate the wonders of God. Moses was not impressed and continued to obey the voice of God. As the plagues grew in intensity, God would not be mocked. After the third plague, however, the Lord made sure that only the Egyptians would suffer through the plagues that followed. This goes to prove that there is a difference between God's people and those that don't know Him. Never had a man been used as mightily of God as with Moses, God confirming his call with signs and wonders. (Ex. 7-12)

The final stage concludes where we settle in, much like concrete settling in to form a great foundation. God forms us into His own image and likeness. At this point we become steadfast and unmovable (1 Cor. 15:58) and a vessel of honor (2 Tim. 2:20), one that He could brag about.

Although thankful that God has taken the time to help me understand what He is trying to do in my life at this moment, I still find myself hating myself more times than not. I cannot believe the things that come my way that cause me to fall so easily. At times I am utterly embarrassed by my lack of resistance, and I feel very much the way I did when I first came to serve God. How could He possibly put up with such immaturity and lack of discipline when I have known Him for so long?

> A bruised reed He will not break, And smoking flax He will not quench . . .
>
> Isaiah 42:3

It takes a minimal amount of effort to break a bruised reed, perhaps even less to quench smoking flax. Yet, the Lord won't even attempt to go there, because His ultimate desire is to give us life and that in more abundance. He knows that in order for us to get back to full strength, we are given choices daily so that we can continue to make the right decisions.

> *And if it seems evil to you to serve the LORD, choose for yourselves this day whom you will serve . . .*
>
> Joshua 24:15

Knowing that the worst part of my evil day was now behind me, I was looking forward to things getting back to normal. Things now could not possibly get any worse, so I thought. I was soon to find out that the writing of this book would bring with it different kind of pressures, ones that proved to be far more overwhelming than what I had just experienced within the last five years. After a couple of months, I began to relish the thought that sometime later in the year the Lord was going to take me home. I tried to begin preparing my children by leaving them subtle hints, but they wanted no part of it.

The chronic pain in my body only added to my misery, and I became a top-notch whiner before the Lord. It all came to a head when in June God decided to call me on the carpet. I was preaching a three-day revival at a church in the area when the horrendous pains that I felt in the stomach area did not allow me to finish. For the next three days, the pains only worsened, but I felt assured from God that it was not unto death. Finally on the third day a little past midnight, I went to the restroom thinking that, if I could just have a bowel movement I would go back to bed and continue to endure the pain. It is then that the Lord spoke to me more clearly than I had ever heard Him in the past. He said, "You have been asking me now for quite some time to die and tonight I am going to give you the choice. Just say the word and in the morning you will be with Me in Paradise."

I began to ponder the offer that was being made and could not believe that God was responding to my petition. Actually I didn't even want to think about it, because I was ready to go. But the presence of the Lord began to overwhelm me, and I began to remember how that I had not even attempted to write this book. I then began to think about how my daughters were not serving God at the moment, and who would it be to get them back to the grace of God? Finally, my thoughts came to my son Timothy, the only one that stayed with me through thick and thin. My passing would truly affect him more adversely than anyone else. So I sheepishly called to the Lord saying that I had decided to stay right where I was. It was then that He lovingly uttered this phrase, "Remember Elder Ross." Immediately I woke up my son and told him that we needed to get to the emergency room as soon as possible. God's message to me rang so very clear, because Elder Ross died of a ruptured appendix. He was my ex-wife's first piano teacher, who decided to ignore the pains that he was feeling in the right stomach area. When he finally did go to the hospital, he was too late and the poison had done its damage, killing him. After several hours and several tests had been taken, I was diagnosed with a ruptured appendix. They admitted me to the hospital with the intentions of draining the fluid with the help of a CAT scan. I was informed that once the CAT scan was done, a catheter would be attached to the area for several days. What actually happened was, once the fluid was drained, God miraculously healed me. I did not need a catheter, and I was allowed to go home two days later. When I asked the doctor why I was able to go home sooner than expected, all he could say is that I had healed much faster than anyone else. I asked them if the appendix had actually burst. He said that it hadn't. I asked then what the fluid that was taken out was. He responded that they didn't know. All he was asking of me is that I return in two months to have the appendix taken out. Yeah, right!

We may think that in trying times, there are no choices at our disposal. Sometimes we just need to look a little deeper and a little harder, and God will make it clear to us what to do. In the meantime, we can put our hope and trust in the one who loves us more than anyone else, the Lord Jesus Christ. And as we put that trust in the Lord, as the Psalmist did, we say:

But I will hope continually, And will praise You yet more and more . . .

Psalm 71:14

Books Available in English

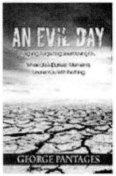  

Libros Disponibles En Español

George Pantages Ministries

George Pantages
Cell 512 785-6324
geopanjr@yahoo.com
Georgepantages.com